Good Crabmeat Recipes 12/98

Louis Evans'
Creole Cookbook

Louis Evans' Creole Cookbook

by Louis Evans

Foreword by Mel Leavitt

Pelican Publishing Company
Gretna 1991

Library of Congress Cataloging-in-Publication Data

Evans, Louis
    [Creole cookbook]
    Louis Evans' Creole cookbook / foreword by Mel Leavitt.
      p. cm.
    Includes index.
    ISBN 0-88289-799-3
    1. Cookery, Creole. I. Title
TX715.E8828 1991
641.59763—dc20   90-20533
                                                  CIP

Manufactured in the United States of America
Published by Pelican Publishing Company, Inc.
1101 Monroe Street, Gretna, Louisiana 70053

Contents

Foreword

Dining in old New Orleans is more than an experience. It is an adventure. This fabled old Creole city always has considered the preparation—and delectation—of fine food a major event, and in the hands of an expert chef, a genuine art form.

When it comes to Creole cooking, master chef Louis Evans was recognized as a true artiste. He was the first black chef in history to be admitted to the exclusive Order of the Golden Toque, restricted to 100 members nationwide. For eighteen years, while executive chef of the Caribbean Room in the Pontchartrain Hotel, Evans' distinctive cuisine consistently was rated four stars or better by almost every major food critic or international/national guidebook on grand restaurants.

Julia Child personally selected Evans as one of only thirteen American master chefs to appear on her thirteen-week special PBS series, "Dinner at Julia's." He rewarded her audience with his own special variation of the classic Louisiana crawfish bisque.

Few chefs have come close to capturing that indescribable "New Orleans taste" that delights the senses and excites the palate. Genuine Creole cooking, according to Leon E. Soniat, Jr. (author of *La Bouche Creole,* also published by Pelican), is a tantalizing mixture. "The recipe for Creole cooking started with the French love of, and skill in, manipulating anything edible into a tasty dish. Then, if you combined this with the Spanish gust for piquancy, the native African ability for developing a slow cooking method to perfection, and the gift of herbs and spices from the Indians, you had the beginning of Creole cooking."

Carried down through generations, it has made New Orleans the only American city to boast its own distinct cuisine. This is not just a few dishes or specialties but a complete indigenous approach to food,and to cooking.

Evans' personal history should serve as an inspiration to anyone who loves to cook. He was born in a sharecropper's cabin in rural Mississippi, one of seven children. His first experience was helping his mother in their modest kitchen. Later, after the family moved to New Orleans, Evans served in the armed forces as a mess hall cook.

Upon graduation from high school, he landed a job in the pantry at Sclafani's highly respected Italian restaurant. In his off-hours, he took cooking courses at Delgado College. For three years he did just about everything, including mopping the restaurant's floors and painting the dining room.

"I was determined to learn everything about cooking and the operation of a restaurant," Evans said. He carried a notepad around constantly. The proprietor, Pete Sclafani, took a liking to him. Every day, from 8 A.M. to 9 P.M., Evans was on the job, mixing salads, learning to make pastas, buying the butchering meat. He literally shadowed Mr. Pete. He became Pete's protégé, almost part of the family. The Sclafanis called him "Sonny" and he became their chief chef.

Evans' ten years of "schooling" paid off handsomely. The legendary hotelier, Lysle Aschaffenburg, owner of one of America's most select residential hotels, the posh Pontchartrain, hired him as a relief cook for the hotel's celebrated Caribbean Room. Situated on St. Charles Avenue, that grand oak-lined boulevard that borders the antebellum Garden District, the Pontchartrain catered to wealthy residents and discriminating celebrities.

Ever-present notepad in hand, Evans rapidly traveled up the ranks under Aschaffenburg's watchful eye. In short order, he became a sous chef, assistant chef and, finally, executive chef.

"I worked one entire year without a day off," said Louis. "I loved it. I was so eager, I ran to work." His eagerness and talent so impressed the owner, Aschaffenburg sent him to the prestigious Prince School in Toronto (1972) and the famous Culinary Institute in Hyde Park, New York (1974).

By the time Lysle Aschaffenburg died in 1982, his handpicked Caribbean Room chef had become a national celebrity. Such megastars as Richard Burton and Mary Martin were regular patrons of both the hotel and the restaurant. Gerald Ford and Henry Kissinger dined there (accompanied by the usual Secret Service men). Yul Brynner, Beverly Sills, and Tom Selleck feasted on Truite Veronique and Evans' imposing Mile High Pie. Truman Capote dined nightly at the Caribbean—and never failed to order Evans' incredible seafood gumbo. In this remarkable and challenging atmosphere, Evans created such exotic dishes as oyster and artichoke soup, red snapper with crawfish sauce, and his succulent crabmeat Biarritz.

Some patrons were particular. The late Lillian Hellman insisted on being seated by the fountain. "Such serenity calms the gastric juices," the playwright said.

Evans' reputation spread. On television, he shared his own cooking secrets with Mike Douglas. He was admitted to the Golden Toque (named after the distinctive tall chef's cap worn by masters of cuisine). In 1986, he was named Chef of the Year in his own vigorously competitive backyard, New Orleans.

In New Orleans, where it is the ritual Monday meal-in-itself, there may be one thousand different ways to cook red beans and rice. In a highly publicized cook off at the Fairmont Hotel, Evans beat out fourteen of the finest chefs in the city for the title: "King of Red Beans." This, in itself, tells you something about the man and his pragmatic approach to cooking.

"I look for things that will work, things that have the right ingredients. I'm no genius, but I am experienced. And I can tell if a recipe is workable. Some people try things that don't work. Good, tested recipes will work for you. And you don't have to be a master chef to pull them off."

Louis Evans was a working chef. Unlike some contemporaries, he did not cook to please himself—he cooked to please his customers. In the kitchen, he moved constantly, checking ingredients, sampling dishes. From time to time, he toured the dining room, checking service and talking to customers.

"Cooking is something you have to feel. Growing up, there were six boys and one girl. The girl was very young so we all took our turn at the stove. You learn by doing when you cook for a large family."

When the Pontchartrain Hotel was sold in 1987, Louis was scooped up by Kabby's restaurant, located in the New Orleans Hilton Riverside and Towers Hotel. This spacious room overlooks the majestic Mississippi River, offering a breathtaking view. Here, Evans' sure grasp of Creole cuisine, especially those unique fresh fish and shellfish dishes, was unrivalled.

"I feel at home at Kabby's," said Chef Evans. "People come from all over the world looking for that special, distinctive New Orleans taste."

Some chefs jealously guard their secrets. Not so with Louis. "Older chefs would never let us apprentices see what they were up to. Why, they'd hide the spice box behind their back...or send you to the icebox for something and, when you came back, it was already fixed."

"A secretive chef," Evans maintained, "is a scared chef...scared somebody would take his job."

In this book, Evans freely shares three decades of hard work, learning, and experience. Good recipes will work and they need not be complicated or off-the-wall. As Julia Child points out, "In the kitchens of complete chefs, time is money, the creation of a recipe is an investment in their future, and correct preparation is vital to their success."

Evans said he learned two things early on. "You can't cook from an office. And just because a recipe looks good on paper, just because a dish goes out to the dining room, doesn't mean it's right." His thoughts on cooking, and his recipes, are so designed.

With Chef Louis looking over your shoulder, so to speak, you may well be delighted at how good a cook you can be...and gratified at how good a cook you are regarded by friends and family.

As we say in New Orleans, "May the next dish be the best dish you have ever cooked in your life...and the next...and the next."

MEL LEAVITT

Acknowledgments

Special thanks to my lovely wife, Annie, for being with me, putting up with the long hours, being so understanding, and raising our three children. I don't think I could have made it without her. Of course, Annie played a large part in keeping the children in line, especially through my leave for months to go back to school. I told my children if raising two girls and one son was that easy I should have had three more. Thanks to my children, Dale B. Evans Jones, Melissa G. Evans, and Roy Glen Evans.

I wish to acknowledge the late Peter Sclafani for giving me a start in cooking and teaching me so much. The late Lysle Aschaffenburg stuck with me through the years and sent me to the CIA, one of the best schools in New York. Thanks also to Mr. Albert, his son. Mr. Paul Buckley, the general manager at the New Orleans Hilton, gave me the opportunity to be the chef at Kabby's. Mr. Leo K. Food and B. M. of the Hilton also were always there when I needed them. Mr. Jeffery Shiffer is my best friend, and I learned so much from him.

Special thanks to Robbie Jean Wiggins, a dear friend who did the typing for this book, and who put up with me for the last couple of years. My close friend, Mrs. Marilyn Barnett, gave me encouragement, and told me how good I am. She would always tell me, "Louis, you can do it." Thanks also to Pelican Publishing Company, and their staff for allowing me to do this book.

Introduction

I've been cooking since 1958 in New Orleans, Louisiana. I was born in a little town in Mississippi: Carlisle. I come from a family of six brothers and one sister, attended New Hymn High School in Pinola, Mississippi, and graduated from Booker T. Washington Senior High School in New Orleans. After cooking for ten years, I went to Toronto and studied at the Prince School, then one year later went to the Culinary Institute of America.

I first started cooking in an Italian restaurant. On a New Year's Eve, I was working on this restaurant (setting tile) and the owner asked me to help wash dishes, so I told him yes. I had never seen so many glasses and dishes. But I stayed until 2:00 in the morning.

The owner asked me that night to come to work for him. I told him I did not want to wash dishes, I had a job setting tile. So he started me out in the pantry and I was excited. He taught me the first thing I ever cooked, which was caramel cup custard. I was impressed. I learned the many ways you can use eggs. The next dish I cooked was bread pudding, with a vanilla sauce.

I was the youngest person behind the line. I was seventeen years old then, and being so young I always had to watch close. They called me "Sonny."

The first thing I had to do when I came to work was vacuum the dinner room, set the pantry, and then I would go and help on prestation. If the pot-wash did not show up, I washed pots. I learned from an Italian lady, who was sixty-seven years old but looked like she was fifty-five. We made twelve gallons of tomato sauce every morning. I would wash the pots, peel the garlic, and chop the onions. If she burned the pots four or five times, I washed them.

The person who used to give me a lot of help was Mrs. Dorothy. At the restaurant, I learned how to cut meat and fish. We used all fresh food, and that stayed with me through my life.

Mr. Sclafani came to the kitchen one morning and I was making the tomato sauce. He walked over and asked me who showed me all the dishes. He liked to come in the kitchen early, so I came in early too. I became his chef, and he sent me to vocational school but I told him that I was learning more from him than at the school. Mr. Sclafani was one of the best cooks I've ever known. I'll never forget him.

Every Sunday when I was growing up I would watch my mother cook; she would use fresh ingredients also. Of course, we made what we cooked—we ground our own cornmeal. From the first day I started cooking, I loved it. No matter how many hours I would spend cooking, it never seemed like I was tired. I would wake up without a clock, no matter what time I got off the night before. I worked from 8:00 in the morning until 9:00 P.M., six days a week, sometimes seven days. Every time I got a chance to learn something, I would work. Whenever I pass this restaurant, I think of all the things I learned. I painted the dinner room, hooked the stove up (the very stove I learned to cook on), hung Sheetrock, and painted the owner's apartment.

I know that God looked over me everyday. Most of my customers liked me. I am good with people; it takes a lot to get me upset. With my cooks, I have a way of knowing when I get someone who doesn't want to do what I want them to do and when this happens I let them go elsewhere.

I don't like changing jobs every year. My first job in a restaurant I stayed eleven years. Then I felt that I needed a change from tomato to Creole, French, and American.

I always worked for a family restaurant. I went to the Pontchartrain Hotel, which was a father and son operation. They had the same idea about fresh meat and vegetables, etc. Mr. Lysle Aschaffenburg there was responsible for me going to CIA in New York. I started working at the Pontchartrain Hotel as a relief chef. Jeffery Shiffer was the general manager who promoted me to sous chef after six weeks on the job. Then, after one year, I became executive chef. There again, I was given the job by Mr. Lysle when I came off my vacation. I never asked how much he was going to pay me. When I took the job I told him that I would do my best and if he did not like it, to call me back. He never called me back except for me to sign my contract.

I served almost eighteen years at the Pontchartrain Hotel. There was always excitement. That's where Mr. Lysle taught me to go out in the dinner room, listen, and talk to the customers. He said, "There are things the customers will tell the chef that they won't tell anyone else. Besides, the customers like to talk to the chef." I have national celebrities I could name as my customers but it would take more time than I have now.

The Julia Child show I did was in Santa Barbara, California. I shipped live crawfish and everything else that I needed. Julia did the main course for the dinner. She had never seen live crawfish, so I showed her how to prepare them by putting salt in cold water and boiling the crawfish. I made a light roux (dark roux is too strong for crawfish bisque). I have used this recipe for over twenty years. I stuffed the crawfish heads and used two-day-old French bread. The recipe for Crawfish Bisque is in this book.

Gumbo is one soup you find in almost every New Orleans restaurant. They're all different. I like to fix Creole and Cajun gumbo, which has filé, sausage, shrimp, oysters, and crabs. Of course, this gumbo has dark roux.

Over the years, my reputation spread on television, nationally and locally. I was asked to be on the "Mike Douglas Show." He wanted a Creole chef to fix shrimp creole. Mr. Albert went with me to California to the studio. When we arrived the guard asked who we wanted to see. Mr. Albert said he was the owner of the Pontchartrain Hotel in New Orleans and the guard let him in. I said who I was, and the guard then asked, "Are these people with you?" I said yes, so he let everyone in. Mr. Albert said to me, "Just goes to show you, it ain't what you own, it's who you are."

I've always been a working chef. I like to get in with my employees and let them ask me questions. This way I get to know them and they learn. I never found anything that I love better than cooking. Before I came to the Hilton, the Meridien Hotel asked me to go to London for three weeks to cook Creole. This was a great experience in my life.

With all the great things in my life, there is one thing that stands out. In 1976, Warren Leruth called me and asked if I would help do a charity for St. Michael's Special School in New Orleans and I said yes. But I never thought it would turn out the way it did. He picked twelve chefs. This has become an annual event, involving two days of cooking demonstrations every January. My first dish for the charity was "Shrimp 21," in a pastry shell. Many great chefs work for the St. Michael's benefit, and I won't forget Sister Lillian, one of the greatest persons I know.

I came from a very poor family. I knew I had no one to give me anything. I was taught never to depend on what someone else had. So in this book, there's over thirty years of experience in the recipes that I am sharing with you.

BON APPETIT

Editor's note: Chef Louis Evans died in New Orleans in 1990, shortly after completing the manuscript for this cookbook.

Louis Evans' Creole Cookbook

Appetizers

An appetizer is the first dish in a restaurant that you order when you dine out, so you expect it to be good. Over the years I have come up with quite a few good ones. Take the Crabmeat Remick. I never served this dish to anyone and I even tried it with a mayonnaise base. The key to it is to get your crabmeat hot and add the sauce last, just enough to get it hot. I used this dish for 17 years at the Pontchartrain Hotel.

At Kabby's, in the Hilton, I give our guests boiled Creole Potatoes with Ravigote Sauce, which I created. Over 75 percent of the recipes in this book I created. The Ham-Stuffed Mushrooms are used a lot. They were developed for a Wedding Special at the Pontchartrain Hotel, along with Creole Oysters Wrapped in Bacon. In New Orleans there is so much seafood you can use catfish chips as I use at Kabby's.

CRABMEAT REMICK

1 lb. lump crabmeat
6 small pieces cooked bacon
½ tsp. dry mustard
½ tsp. paprika

½ tsp. celery salt
½ cup chili sauce
1 tsp. tarragon vinegar
½ cup mayonnaise

Divide the crabmeat into 6 portions; pile into individual ramekins. Heat in oven for 8 minutes at 350°.

While waiting for crabmeat to heat, proceed with making sauce. Blend together all dry ingredients. Add chili sauce and tarragon vinegar; mix well. Then blend in mayonnaise.

When crabmeat is very hot, place a piece of crisp bacon in the middle of each ramekin and on top spread the Remick Sauce, just enough to cover. Return ramekins to oven just for a few seconds and serve immediately. (The Remick Sauce will separate if dish is left inside oven too long.)

CRAB 'N CHEESE SANDWICH

Toast two pieces of bread (per serving). Cut one piece into a square and the other into two triangles. Coat the toast with tartar sauce.

FILLING

1 lb. crabmeat (jumbo lump)
Dash Worcestershire sauce
Enough mayonnaise for
    mixture so it is not dry mix

Salt and pepper to taste
Dash Tabasco
Dash lemon juice

Mix filling ingredients and put on top of the square piece of toast with a slice of American cheese. Put into oven until cheese becomes golden brown (350°), about 5 to 8 minutes. Garnish with remaining toast.

OLIVE CRAB MOUSSE

1 cup canned, pitted, ripe olives
2 envelopes unflavored gelatin
¾ cup cold water
2 tbsp. lemon juice
½ tsp. Worcestershire sauce
1 cup catsup
2 cups dairy sour cream

1 10-oz. pkg. frozen asparagus spears
½ cup mayonnaise
½ tsp. salt
Few drops Tabasco
7½ oz. crabmeat
Salad greens, ripe olives, and tiny pickled green tomatoes for garnish

Slice olives. Cook asparagus just until tender; drain. Sprinkle gelatin over water; stir over low heat until dissolved. Add slowly to mayonnaise, beating briskly. Blend in lemon juice, salt, Worcestershire sauce, Tabasco sauce, and catsup. Drain and flake crabmeat. Reserve a few asparagus and fold the rest into gelatin mixture with some of the olives, and all the sour cream and crab. Chill until slightly thickened. Place reserved olives in bottom of 6–cup mold. Cover with a little thickened gelatin. Arrange asparagus spears tips down against sides of mold. Chill quickly, then spoon in remaining gelatin mixture. Chill until firm. Unmold and garnish. Serves 8–10.

SEAFOOD MOLD

I serve this Seafood Mold at Kabby's for Sunday Brunch. When I first made this recipe I used crawfish and crabmeat. I found out later that substituting red snapper or grouper (firm fish) for the crabmeat made the mold come out better. You can mold this in individual servings and put them on Melba Rounds or you can use the little soufflé cups. All you really want is to have something to sit it in when you put it in the freezer.

½ lb. crabmeat
½ lb. crawfish
½ bell pepper, chopped
1 qt. seafood stock
½ cup diced red pepper
2 oz. gelatin
1 tsp. salt

2 oz. cold water
2 oz. green pepper sauce
¼ cup chopped yellow onion
½ bunch green onion, chopped
1 clove garlic, chopped
3 oz. yellow mustard

Sauté yellow onion, bell pepper, and garlic together for 5-6 minutes. Add seafood stock, crawfish tails, green pepper sauce, crabmeat, salt, chopped red pepper, green onion, and yellow mustard. Mix gelatin with cold water; turn off heat and add gelatin. Put in 1½-quart mold dish or individual molds and put in freezer for 6-8 hours before serving.

SPINACH MOLD

I use this dish for Sunday Brunch at Kabby's in the Hilton. Also, this can be made in small molds. This has to be the best mold I ever made. I found a way to get people to eat more spinach.

2½ lb. chopped spinach, drained
½ lb. cooked bacon, chopped
1 oz. green pepper sauce
1½ oz. gelatin

1½ oz. cold water
1½ cups sour cream
1 pt. chicken stock
4 boiled eggs, cut in half
1 bunch green onions, chopped

Put chicken stock on burner to get hot. Add sour cream, chopped bacon, green pepper sauce, and chopped green onions; mix well. Mix gelatin with cold water and stir. Turn off heat and add gelatin. Put boiled eggs in bottom of 1½-quart mold dish with the yolk down. Pour enough of the mix to cover the eggs, put in freezer, let set. When firm, take out of freezer.

Mix the spinach with rest of the mix and pour on top of the mix that you take out of the freezer. Once you smooth it out, put the mold in the freezer for 4-6 hours, and unmold on tray. Garnish with sour cream rose.

INDIVIDUAL QUICHES
LORRAINES

1 egg, lightly beaten
¾ cup milk
Pinch salt
4 slices bacon, fried crisp
 and crumbled
18 tiny tart shells (below)

5 tbsp. grated parmesan
 cheese
Dash cayenne pepper
3 tbsp. chopped chives
 (or onion)

Mix together egg and cheese; add milk, salt, and pepper. Divide bacon and chives (or onion) among tart shells, then fill each with egg-cheese-milk mixture. Bake in a moderately hot oven (375°) for 20 minutes. Serve hot.

TART PASTRY

1 cup flour
⅓ cup shortening

Pinch salt
About ¼ cup ice water

Sift together flour and salt and crumble in shortening with fingers or a pastry blender. Add enough water, cutting it with a knife a little at a time, to make a dough that is not too soft. Form into a ball. Cover it and chill in refrigerator for at least 1 hour.

For individual quiches, grease 18 tiny tartlet molds. Roll out dough on a floured board about ⅛ inch thick and cut into circles that will fill molds. Put a circle of foil or waxed paper in the bottom of each over the pastry, and fill with dry beans or rice and chill for 15 minutes in refrigerator. Bake in hot oven (400°) for 15 minutes. Discard beans or rice and paper or foil circles and fill (as described above). Serves 18.

CHICKEN MOLD

1 pt. chicken stock
1 bunch green onions,
  chopped
2 ribs celery, chopped
2 oz. Worcestershire sauce
1½ cups sour cream
1 oz. gelatin

1 oz. cold water
1½ lb. turkey breast,
  chopped
1 oz. yellow mustard
1 cup sliced mushrooms
1 oz. Creole mustard

Put chicken stock on burner to get hot and add celery, green onions, Worcestershire sauce, Creole mustard, yellow mustard, mushrooms, sour cream, and turkey breast. Let come to a boil. Mix gelatin with cold water; turn off heat, add gelatin, and mold. Set in freezer for 4-6 hours.

SHRIMP ASPIC MOLD

1 lb. shrimp, chopped
6 chicken bouillon cubes
2 tsp. ground allspice
¼ cup lemon juice
1 rib celery, chopped
½ bell pepper
24-oz. can tomato juice

24-oz. can V-8 juice
2 oz. green pepper sauce
4 oz. gelatin
½ yellow onion, chopped
1 cup black olives, chopped
4 oz. cold water

Sauté shrimp, celery, onion, and bell pepper together until shrimp turn pink. Add tomato juice, green pepper sauce, V-8 juice, olives, allspice, lemon juice, and bouillon cubes. Mix well and let come to a boil, then reduce heat. Mix gelatin with cold water and take off heat. Add gelatin. Put in mold dish and set in freezer for 4 hours. Once you turn out the mold, you can garnish with sour cream on top of each serving.

RED SNAPPER OR TROUT MOLD

Put water into bottom of fish poacher. Add black pepper, salt, onion, celery, juice of ½ lemon, and 1 bay leaf. Boil until soft. Put in fish (2 or 3 according to size) until cooked (do not let it lose its firmness). Remove fish from water (be sure to keep water). Peel fish skin and pick meat off with fork after it is cold. Add 1 cup of mayonnaise that is seasoned with juice of ½ lemon, a bit of Worcestershire sauce, drop or two of Tabasco, and 1½ tsp. soy sauce. Now soak 1 envelope of gelatin in ⅓ of fish water and add to fish and mayonnaise mixture. Put in 1½-quart mold; refrigerate for 2 hours.

Use about 1 cup of mayonnaise seasoned as the other. Add ⅓ cup of fish water, add capers, and serve separately as sauce.

CREOLE OYSTERS WRAPPED IN BACON

½ gallon oysters
1 bunch parsley, chopped
15 oz. Worcestershire sauce
3 lb. bread crumbs
1 tbsp. salt

8 bay leaves
1½ tbsp. white pepper
3 lb. bacon
1 lb. all-purpose flour

Egg Wash: 1 qt. milk, 8 whole eggs. Beat together.

Pour Worcestershire sauce into a large pot. Add the oysters and bay leaves and let come to a boil. Turn off heat and let sit for 30 minutes, then drain.

Cut bacon into 2-inch pieces and wrap around oysters with a toothpick. Place in egg wash. Mix bread crumbs, salt, pepper, parsley, and flour together, then coat oysters with this mixture. Fry in hot grease (275°) until brown. Serve. Makes 4 dozen.

TROUT MOUSSES WITH
MADEIRA TRUFFLE SAUCE
(Mousse de Truite Perigueux)

In batches, in a food processor fitted with the steel blade or in a blender, purée 10 ounces of trout fillets or salmon trout fillets, skinned and cut into 1-inch pieces.

Add 3 ounces of beef marrow, 3 chicken livers, trimmed and quartered, and salt and pepper to taste and blend the mixture until it is combined. Blend in 6 whole eggs, two at a time, and 5 egg yolks, and pour in 1 cup scalded milk.

Blend the mixture, strain it through a fine sieve into a metal bowl, and chill it, covered, for 2 hours.

Divide the mixture among 12 well-buttered 2-inch dariole molds, 2 inches deep (available at kitchenware specialty shops). Arrange the molds in a baking pan, and add enough hot water to the pan to reach halfway up the sides of the molds.

Cover the pan with foil and bake the mousses in a preheated moderately slow oven (325°) for 25-30 minutes, or until they are firm. Run a thin knife around the inside of each mold and invert the mousses onto a heated platter. Cover the mousses with 2½ cups Sauce Perigueux. Serves 12.

SAUCE PERIGUEUX

In a saucepan combine 1⅓ cups Madeira Sauce (see below) with 1 tbsp. minced black truffle and a little of the truffle liquor. Simmer the sauce over low heat for 5 minutes and swirl in 1 tbsp. softened butter. Makes about 1⅓ cups.

MADEIRA SAUCE

In a saucepan reduce 2 cups brown sauce over high heat to 1 cup. Add ⅓ cup Sercial Madeira, bring the sauce to the boiling point, and remove the pan from the heat. Makes about 1⅓ cups.

OYSTERS BIENVILLE

1 stick butter	4 doz. oysters on half-shell
1 cup finely chopped green onions	1½ cups finely chopped raw shrimp
1 cup finely chopped yellow onions	1 tsp. salt
6 oz. fresh raw mushrooms, finely chopped	½ tsp. white pepper
2 tbsp. lemon juice	⅛ tsp. cayenne pepper
¼ cup flour	4 egg yolks
2 cups chicken consommé	¼ cup whipping cream
1 cup dry white wine	8 pie pans
	3 lb. ice cream salt

TOPPING MIX

¾ cup grated imported parmesan cheese
¾ cup clarified butter
½ cup dry bread crumbs (plain)
Paprika

In heavy 3-quart pot, melt butter. Add green and yellow onions. Sauté gently until wilted. Add mushrooms and lemon juice and continue to sauté, stirring frequently, for about ½ hour. Do not allow to brown. Remove pan from heat and sprinkle flour over contents. Stir until well blended.

Return to heat, and over gentle heat, slowly stir in consommé and white wine. Raise heat and continue cooking and stirring about 10 minutes until sauce has thickened. Add shrimp, salt, pepper, and cayenne, and cook 5 more minutes. Remove from heat.

Beat together egg yolks and whipping cream. Add a little warm sauce to yolk combination, then stir well back into mixture. Partially fill pie pans with ice cream salt. Pour off excess liquid from each oyster; place oyster and shell on ice cream salt (6 to a pan).

Place in preheated 350° oven for 10 minutes. Remove pans from oven. Tip each shell to remove excess liquid and turn oven to 500°. Cover each oyster with sauce. Top each with mixture of cheese, bread crumbs, and butter. Sprinkle with paprika. Bake at 500° until brown, about 10-15 minutes.

SHRIMP REMOULADE

3 tbsp. hot prepared mustard
½ cup tarragon vinegar
½ tsp. cayenne pepper
½ cup green onions, finely minced
1 clove garlic, finely minced
1 cup salad oil

1 tbsp. horseradish
1 tsp. salt
1 tbsp. paprika
½ cup celery, finely minced
2 tbsp. catsup
2 lb. cooked, cleaned shrimp

Combine all ingredients except shrimp, blending well. Pour over shrimp and chill well before serving on shredded lettuce. Serves 8.

CATFISH CHIPS

8 oz. catfish fillets, sliced thin
1 oz. Creole mustard
1 tsp. parsley, chopped

¼ tsp. Tabasco sauce
4 oz. creamed cornmeal
1 egg

Mix mustard, Tabasco, and egg together. Add catfish fillets. Let sit at least 1 hour. Dredge catfish in creamed cornmeal and deep fry until golden brown, about 5-6 minutes. Garnish with parsley.

TOMATO ASPIC

This is an old recipe. I used to serve this mold with egg salad and the only difference was that I used chopped shrimp. On occasion I would use whole shrimp and mold the egg salad in the center of the aspic ring. You can buy the little ring. Just put the mixture in the same way and turn it out, placing the egg salad in the center and large shrimp (that have been boiled) around the aspic.

2 envelopes unflavored
  gelatin
2 cups tomato juice
2 tsp. vinegar or lemon juice
⅛ tsp. pepper
Pinch sugar
Shrimp Remoulade (see
  index for recipe)
Lettuce
Sliced tomatoes

Chopped fresh dill
1 cup cold water
2 tsp. onion juice
1 tsp. salt
⅛ tsp. hot pepper sauce
1 cup cooked artichoke
  hearts or asparagus,
  chopped (optional)
Sliced avocados
Sliced hard-boiled eggs

Soak gelatin in cold water. Heat tomato juice to boiling. Pour over gelatin, stirring to dissolve. Stir in onion juice, vinegar, salt, pepper, hot pepper sauce, and sugar. Fold in artichoke hearts or asparagus. Turn into a 3-cup ring mold (or 4-cup ring mold, if artichokes or asparagus are used). Chill until firm. Unmold on large platter. Fill center of mold with drained Shrimp Remoulade. Surround with lettuce, avocado, tomato, and egg slices. Sprinkle with chopped fresh dill. Garnish with mayonnaise, if desired. Serves 6.

COCKTAIL CHEESE MIX

½ lb. cream cheese
1 small onion
Few celery tops
3 springs parsley, finely
   chopped
Olive oil
Paprika

¼ lb. blue cheese, grated
   (about ½ cup)
3 drops Tabasco
Salt and freshly ground
   pepper
Melba toast

Mash cream cheese with a fork until very soft and combine with blue cheese. Add chopped ingredients and seasonings (except oil and paprika). Mix in a little olive oil drop-by-drop to make a good spreading consistency. Put into serving bowl and sprinkle with paprika. Chill in refrigerator for an hour or more before using. Serve with Melba toast. The flavor is greatly improved if mixture is kept in the refrigerator for several days. Makes 1 pint.

CHEESE STRAWS

1 cup grated sharp cheese
4½ tbsp. milk
Pinch cayenne
¾ cup flour

3 tbsp. butter
½ tsp. salt
1½ cups fine soft
   bread crumbs

Preheat the oven to 400°. Grease baking sheet. Mix the cheese and butter, add remaining ingredients, mix, and knead until smooth. Roll on a lightly floured pastry cloth to about ⅜ inch thickness and cut into strips that are 6 inches long and ½ inch wide.

Place on prepared baking sheets. If desired, one quarter of the strips may be shaped into rings with the overlapping ends brushed with egg before pressing them together. Bake until lightly browned, about 12 minutes. Makes about 36 straws.

CHEESE BALL

2 oz. chopped almonds
24 oz. blue cheese
24 oz. cream cheese
1 tbsp. chopped white onion

2 oz. Worcestershire sauce
¾ oz. Tabasco sauce
2 tbsp. chopped chives

Mix all ingredients except almonds. Shape into a ball. Roll in chopped almonds.

SWISS CHEESE TARTLETS

Pastry for 2-crust pie
⅔ cup milk
1 tsp. flour
½ tsp. salt

4 eggs
½ lb. Swiss cheese, grated
¼ tsp. pepper

Roll out pastry dough thinly, cut into small rounds, and fit into tiny tartlet pans. Bake in a 400° oven until pastry is light brown but not quite done. Remove from oven and cool in pans. Beat eggs slightly; add milk, then grated cheese, flour, salt, and pepper and blend. Fill pastry shells three-quarters full, return to oven, and bake at 425° for about 12-15 minutes or until set. Do not overbake as they will dry out. Makes 2 dozen.

GRITS SOUFFLE

1 lb. grits
2 eggs

½ lb. sharp cheddar cheese, grated

Cook grits according to package directions. Add cheese while grits are hot, and allow cheese to melt. Stir well. When cool, add eggs, well beaten, and cook in 350°-oven for 20 minutes. Serve 15.

CHICKEN LIVER PATE

1 lb. livers, chicken or duck
2 sticks butter
¼ cup chopped green onions
¼ cup cognac
⅛ tsp. freshly ground
black pepper
⅛ tsp. thyme

¾ cup sliced mushrooms
(save several for garnish)
1 tsp. salt
⅛ tsp. cayenne pepper
¼ tsp. powdered allspice
Chopped parsley for garnish

Wash, dry, and chop livers. Sauté mushrooms in butter for 5 minutes. Remove mushrooms with a slotted spoon and set aside. Sauté onions in same pan and cook 5 minutes. Add livers to pan, stir, and cook until still barely pink inside, about 5 minutes. Put into blender; add mushrooms, cognac, and seasonings. If mixture is too thick, add more melted butter (1 to 2 tbsp.). Pack in crocks or a mold and chill. Serve in crock or unmold and decorate with parsley and mushrooms. Freezes well. Serves 18.

VELVET CHICKEN LIVER PATE

½ lb. chicken livers
⅓-½ cup chicken broth
Salt, pepper, and seasoned
salt to taste
2 tbsp. dry sherry
Parsley

2 tbsp. melted butter
2 hard-boiled eggs, chopped
2 3-oz. pkg. cream cheese,
softened
Stuffed olives

Sauté livers in butter about 10 minutes or until just tender. Stir in broth, and swirl in pan a minute; then put in container of electric blender. Add eggs, and blend until smooth. Combine seasonings and cream cheese; add to liver mixture along with sherry, blending well. Put paté in an oiled mold or bowl. Chill. Unmold and garnish with olives and parsley. Serves 8.

HOT DEVILED BACON AND CHEESE CANAPES

⅓ lb. bacon
¼ lb. sharp cheese
Dash cayenne pepper
Parsley

1 large onion
1 tsp. prepared mustard
Cocktail crackers

Put bacon, onion, and cheese through coarse cutter of a meat grinder. Add mustard and cayenne and mix all together. Spread on cocktail crackers and broil until cheese melts. Serve hot, garnished with parsley. Makes 2 dozen.

BACON ROLL-UPS

¼ cup butter or margarine
1½ cups packaged herb-
    seasoned stuffing
½-⅔ lb. sliced bacon
Cherry tomatoes

½ cup water
1 egg, slightly beaten
¼ lb. hot or mild bulk pork
    sausage
Parsley

Melt butter in water in a saucepan; add to stuffing, mixing well. Add egg and sausage; blend thoroughly. Chill 1 hour for easier handling. Then shape into small oblongs, about the size of pecans. Cut bacon slices into thirds. Wrap each piece of stuffing mixture with bacon and fasten with a wooden pick. Place on a rack in a shallow pan. Bake at 375° for 35 minutes or until brown and crisp, turning at halfway point in cooking. Drain on paper towels and serve hot. Garnish with cherry tomatoes and parsley. Makes about 3 dozen.

HAM-STUFFED MUSHROOMS

1 cup finely chopped
  country ham
1 tbsp. Major Grey's
  Chutney, minced
14 (about) small to medium
  mushrooms, stemmed

Onions, minced
1 generous tbsp. Dijon
  mustard
1 tsp. vinegar
Sour cream and mayonnaise
  (to bind)

Combine all ingredients except mushrooms. Mound in mushroom caps and chill until ready to serve. (Can be prepared several hours ahead.) Serves 4-6 as hors d'oeuvres.

STUFFED MUSHROOM CAPS

100 mushroom caps,
  precooked
¼ tsp. salt
¼ tsp. curry powder
¼ tsp. thyme
2 pt. milk
2 bay leaves

5 oz. sherry wine
2 lb. crabmeat
4 oz. butter
2 oz. all-purpose flour
½ bunch green onions,
  finely chopped

Heat milk. In another pot, melt butter. Add flour and mix well. Add hot milk, mix well, and cook for 5 minutes on slow heat.

In another pot, heat sherry wine and green onions. Reduce to half; turn off heat. Mix into cream sauce, along with curry powder, thyme, bay leaves, salt, and crabmeat. Stuff mushrooms with this mixture and bake at 350° for 10 minutes. Serves 30-35.

SNAILS BAKED IN BRIE BUTTER

**40 large mushroom caps,
  half-cooked**

**40 French Helix snails
Brie butter (below)**

Drain the cooked mushrooms well and place snails in them. Cover snails completely with Brie butter and place in oven-proof dish. Bake at 375° for 10 minutes or until butter starts to brown. Serve immediately; garnish with parsley.

BRIE BUTTER

**1-2 kg. herb brie, ring
  removed
2 oz. minced garlic
3 egg yolks
1 lb. butter, unsalted**

**1 tbsp. black pepper,
  freshly ground
2 oz. Pernod
2 tbsp. chives (fresh)**

Beat cheese, butter, liquor, and garlic together until smooth. Add all remaining ingredients and beat until smooth. Refrigerate.

BUTTERMILK BISCUITS

**1 lb. all-purpose flour
⅓ cup baking powder
¼ pt. milk
1 tsp. salt**

**¾ cup shortening
⅓ cup sugar
¾ pt. buttermilk**

Mix all ingredients together and let stand 4 hours. Roll the dough out about ⅛" thick and cut with biscuit cutter. Place on greased baking pan and bake at 350° for 35 minutes. These biscuits have been famous for years at the Pontchartrain. Makes 2 dozen.

Soups

I love to make soup, but creamed soup is not one of my favorites. Some people like it, so I have to serve my customers what they want. Take crab and corn chowder. It's one of the most popular at Kabby's, in the Hilton. It's made with fresh corn, live crabs, heavy cream, diced red pepper, and it's very delectable.

Chicken soup I've been making for over twenty-six years, from my very first job as a cook, at Sclafani's Restaurant. I call the soup "get-well soup" because every time Mr. Peter Sclafani was feeling bad he would ask me to cook some chicken soup. Of course, when I prepared it, I made a large pot because everyone wanted some. I used veal and fried it for about 3¾–4 hours; it was great. The late Peter Sclafani was a great cook but he never put the chicken noodle soup on the menu, and I never asked why. Of course, I used the recipe when I went to the Pontchartrain Hotel.

There I would change soup everyday except Tuesday and Saturday. When I fixed homemade vegetable soup, my customers would buy it by the gallon. I always had a good feel for soup. I've had good teachers along the way.

CRAB AND CORN CHOWDER

¾ cup cooking oil
6 cups corn and crab stock
  (below)
1 lb. whole kernel corn
1 fresh diced potato
Salt and pepper
¾ cup all-purpose flour

½ lb. lump crabmeat
½ diced red bell pepper
2½ cups heavy cream
Dash Tabasco sauce
¼ bunch chopped green
  onion tops

Put oil in 5-qt saucepan. Heat. Add flour. Stir. Add 6 cups hot crab stock. Bring to a boil. Stir with wire whisk. Cook for 5 minutes. Add remaining ingredients, except cream and green onions. Cook for 10 minutes, then add cream. Add green onions last. Serves 8.

CORN AND CRAB STOCK

2 ribs celery
½ green bell pepper
3 bay leaves
½ tsp. oregano leaves
1 lb. whole kernel corn
12 cups water

½ yellow onion
1 whole carrot
1 tsp. thyme leaf
½ tsp. basil leaf
4 whole fresh crabs

Grind all ingredients without water. Add to water. Cook 25 minutes. Strain.

CRAWFISH BISQUE

Crawfish Bisque is an old Creole favorite at Kabby's. I have it on my menu. When I worked for the Pontchartrain, I served it about once a week because I offered a different soup everyday. In 1984, Julia Child did a show called "Dinner at Julia's." she invited me to do Crawfish Bisque. This is the same recipe I did on her show. I used a light roux when I made it because a dark roux will take the flavor from the crawfish. Most people put so much cayenne pepper that you don't really taste the crawfish. I used a green pepper sauce made by Taper Brand. It gives more flavor than heat—you taste the pepper afterward. *Tip*: to purge live crawfish, put them in a large pot with cold water to cover and ½ cup salt per gallon. Let set about ½ hour, then change the water and repeat about four times.

5 lb. raw crawfish	**1 clove garlic, finely chopped**
1 gallon water	**½ bell pepper, finely chopped**
3 lemons, cut in quarters	**½ white onion, finely chopped**
2 tbsp. salt	**1 rib celery, finely chopped**
6 tbsp. shortening	**3 bay leaves**
6 tbsp. all-purpose flour	**½ tsp. chicken base**
½ tsp. sweet basil	**1 tsp. thyme**
½ tsp. cayenne pepper	**½ tsp. green pepper sauce**
2 tbsp. tomato purée	**2 tbsp. chopped parsley**
½ tsp. caramel coloring	

Place raw crawfish in cold water with ½ cup salt added. Allow crawfish to remain in the water for 25 minutes (this is called purging); then wash them off well. Cook in 1 gallon of water with 3 lemons and 2 tbsp. salt until they come to a boil; shut off heat and drain, saving the water. Peel the crawfish tails and save the heads.

In another heavy pot place 6 tbsp. shortening and 6 tbsp. flour. Cook over medium heat until browned. Add garlic, bell pepper, celery, and onion, and cook for 5 minutes. Then add crawfish and 1 gallon reserved crawfish stock, tomato purée, thyme, sweet basil, bay leaves, green pepper sauce, cayenne pepper, chicken base, and caramel coloring. Cook for 30 to 45 minutes. Add the stuffed crawfish heads (see following recipe) and simmer 15-20 minutes. Garnish with parsley. Makes 1½ gallons.

STUFFING FOR CRAWFISH HEADS

½ **bell pepper, finely chopped**
1 **small bunch green onions, chopped**
3 **small hard French loaves**
½ **clove garlic, finely chopped**
3 **eggs**
½ **tsp. thyme**
½ **tsp. salt**
½ **tsp. chicken base**

½ **white onion, finely chopped**
½ **lb. butter**
¾ **lb. peeled crawfish tails**
2 **bay leaves**
½ **tsp. cayenne pepper**
1 **tbsp. chopped parsley**
1 **tsp. Worcestershire sauce**
1 **rib celery, chopped**

Soak the French loaves in some water; then, squeeze the water out. Let drain. In another pot, melt the butter. Add garlic, green onion, bell pepper, parsley, white onion, and celery and cook until the vegetables are tender. Add the crawfish, French bread, bay leaves, cayenne pepper, Worcestershire, chicken base, salt, and thyme and mix well. Add the 3 eggs and mix well. Place in a heated oven (375°) and cook for 25 minutes. Cool. Stuff the crawfish heads with the mixture.

OYSTER CHOWDER SOUP

2 pt. oysters
2 cups chopped onions
½ cup margarine
1 tbsp. chopped parsley
1 tbsp. thyme
1 tsp. white pepper
1 tsp. garlic powder

1 qt. chicken stock
12 oz. heavy cream
1 cup flour
2 cups diced potatoes
4 bay leaves
1 tsp. salt

In medium pot, bring oysters and chicken stock to boil. Skim the top and reduce heat. In another pot, put margarine (melted); add flour and mix well. Add chopped onion, garlic powder, and diced potatoes. Pour the oyster mixture in, mix well, and add thyme and bay leaves. Cook for 15 minutes. Then add heavy cream, parsley, salt, and pepper. Simmer for 10 minutes and serve. Serves 10-12.

OYSTER BROTH

Oysters are served many ways in New Orleans. This recipe was given to me by the late Lysle Aschaffenburg at the Pontchartrain Hotel. Even if you don't like oysters, you would like this broth. At the Pontchartrain we used this on all the special party meals. As the demand grew for it, Mr. Aschaffenburg used it in the spring and the fall because oysters in the summer are milkier.

This broth has no cream in it, as you will read in the recipe. It is not on the menu at Kabby's, but it can be made on request. Mr. Aschaffenburg would call me when he wasn't feeling well and ask me to make oyster broth for him and send it up to his room.

½ gallon oysters
1 white onion
2 pieces celery (not whole
  stalk)
½ lb. butter

2 oz. flour
2 bay leaves
½ gallon water
Salt and pepper to taste
Parsley

Chop onion and celery. Sauté together in pan with butter (do not brown). Add flour, water, oysters, and bay leaves. Bring to boil. Simmer 10 minutes. Add salt and pepper to taste. Strain and serve with parsley. Serves 10.

OYSTER AND ARTICHOKE SOUP

½ gallon oysters
½ lb. butter
1 tsp. salt
¾ tsp. thyme
½ bunch green onions
2 cans artichoke hearts
  (8-10 count)
¾ tsp. Worcestershire sauce
½ gallon water

1 cup white wine
¾ tsp. white pepper
1 rib celery
¼ lb. all-purpose flour
3 bay leaves
1 clove garlic, chopped
½ medium onion, finely
  chopped

Place oysters and water in a 2-gallon pot. Add bay leaves, artichoke hearts (chopped fine), salt, pepper, Worcestershire, and thyme. Bring to a boil. Skim off top, and add cup of white wine. In another pot, melt butter, add chopped onion, garlic, celery, and green onion, and cook until the vegetables are tender. Add flour and cook for 3 minutes on low heat. Then add oyster mix and cook for 10 minutes, stirring constantly, and serve. Makes 1 gallon.

TURTLE SOUP AMONTILLADO

Turtle Soup is one of the old Creole soups. Some Creoles call it "Cowan." Cowan is more of a stew. Some restaurants have used and still use what they call Mock Turtle Soup, meaning they don't use all turtle meat. They use veal, or pork. All turtle costs about six to seven dollars a pound.

This recipe I have used for over twenty-five years and I serve it at Kabby's. You may find it a little spicy. I use the sherry wine amontillado, and also a dark roux. As you may notice, I include allspice, clove, thyme, bay leaf, beef, and chicken stock. I make this soup one day and serve it the next. This is to let the grease come to the top, and the flavor is better.

2 lb. turtle meat	1 large onion, chopped
4 bay leaves	2 cloves garlic, chopped
1 cup tomato sauce	3 tbsp. flour
3 tbsp. oil	8 oz. sherry wine
1 tbsp. Worcestershire sauce	(amontillado)
½ orange	½ lemon, sliced
4 whole allspice	3 hard-boiled eggs
1 tsp. cayenne pepper	1 tbsp. salt
2 qt. water	2 ribs celery, chopped
1 tsp. caramel color	1 tbsp. thyme leaves

In gallon pot (make sure that the pot is heavy) put the oil and let it get hot. Then stir in flour to make a roux. When roux is brown, add garlic, celery, and onion. Mix well, then add tomato sauce, caramel color, and turtle meat. Reduce the heat, stirring constantly.

Add 2 qt. water, cayenne pepper, salt, allspice, Worcestershire sauce, bay leaves, thyme leaves, orange, lemon slice and mix well. Cook for 1 hour and 15 minutes on medium heat. Remove from heat and set aside for 30 minutes before serving. Skim off grease. Soup is better when served the next day. Serve with chopped egg, and sherry wine (dry sherry). Makes 1 gallon.

GUMBO

In New Orleans, Gumbo is fixed many ways—with roux, without roux, with sausage, rabbit, or squirrel. Everyone has their own way of preparing Gumbo. The Creole people start with filé, okra, and seafood. The Cajuns add sausage and oysters. Then you have Rabbit Gumbo, which is sometimes called Creole Gumbo. Every chef you talk to tells you a different way to cook Creole Gumbo. Sometimes the Creoles cook Cajun Gumbo and say it's Creole! Anyway, I hope you try this recipe. I have used it for over 20 years.

¼ yellow onion, finely chopped
¼ bell pepper
½ tsp. chicken base
½ pint oysters
6 hard crabs, cut in pieces
4 oz. peanut oil
3 bay leaves
½ cup tomato purée
¼ tsp. caramel color
6 oz. andouille sausage, diced
5 oz. smoked sausage, diced
2 cloves garlic, chopped

3 tbsp. cold water
1 rib celery, finely chopped
¼ bunch green onion, finely chopped
¾ lb. cut okra
1 lb. shrimp
3 oz. flour
1 tsp. thyme leaves
½ cup broken tomatoes
1 tsp. cayenne pepper
1 tbsp. gumbo filé
1 pt. chicken stock
2 lb. shrimp

Make stock with shrimp peel, hard crabs, and chicken stock. Add chicken base, cook 30 minutes, skim off the top, and strain. In heavy pot make a roux with the oil and flour until brown, then add garlic, celery, bell pepper, green onion, and yellow onion. Cook for 10 minutes; add shrimp, cut okra and thyme leaves. Mix well, then add tomato purée, tomatoes, bay leaves, and both sausages. Add the stock and mix well. Add oysters, crabs, caramel color, and cayenne pepper. Cook for 30 minutes, skim off the top. Mix the gumbo filé with cold water and add to soup. Cook for 10 minutes more. Serve with rice. Makes 2 gallons.

HERBES GUMBO

½ bunch green onions
1 bunch green cabbage
1 bunch radish tops
1 bunch chickory
1 bunch parsley
1 bunch carrot tops
1 bunch beet tops
1 bunch watercress
1 bunch spinach
1 bunch turnip greens
1 bunch mustard greens
1 bunch collard greens
1 gallon water

Cayenne pepper
Salt and pepper
2 whole allspice
2 whole cloves
2 sprigs thyme
2 bay leaves
1 large white onion,
   chopped
2 tbsp. shortening
1 lb. lean veal, diced
1 lb. ham, diced
2 cloves garlic, chopped

Wash all greens and remove all stems or hard centers. Boil greens together in cold water for 2 hours. Strain the greens and save the water. Chop greens finely. Sauté the ham, veal, and garlic in shortening with onion until brown. Add greens, bay leaves, thyme, cloves, allspice, salt, pepper, cayenne, and water from greens. Cook over low heat for 1½ hours. Serves 10-12.

SHRIMP STOCK

1 rib celery
2 gallons water
1 medium onion, chopped

Shrimp shells from 10 lb.
   shrimp
2 bay leaves

Put all ingredients together. Let come to a boil; turn heat down to simmer until it has reduced to ½ gallon. Strain. *Suggestion*: When you peel shrimp, from time to time save the shells and put in freezer. Makes 1 gallon.

SHRIMP BISQUE

2 lb. peeled shrimp
1 pt. half & half cram
1 small white onion
1 small piece of green onion
Salt to taste
3 oz. flour

½ gallon chicken stock
2 oz. white wine
1 small piece of celery
Dash white pepper
½ lb. butter
Dash thyme

Finely chop all vegetables. Sauté in butter. Add flour and cook for 5 minutes on low heat. Add chicken stock. Chop shrimp finely and add to the chicken stock. Add salt, pepper, thyme, and white wine. Cook for half an hour on low heat. Heat cream in a separate saucepan, then stir in with the rest of ingredients. Turn heat off immediately. Serves 10.

FISH STOCK

5 lb. fish bone,
    mixed with head
1 medium yellow onion,
    chopped

2 gal. water
2 carrots, chopped
2 ribs celery, chopped
2 bay leaves

Put all the above in a pot. Let come to a boil, reduce to simmer, and cook until ¾ gallon. Strain. *Suggestion:* When making stock, the best fish is red snapper (use the head). Some dishes may require a light stock, and you can use trout, pompano, or other fish.

MUSHROOM AND BARLEY SOUP

4 oz. diced mushrooms
2 large onions
1 red pepper
3 stalks celery
3 carrots
1 tsp. pepper, freshly ground

1 tsp. salt
3 lb. short ribs of beef
1 cup medium barley
3 tomatoes, quartered
3 qt. water

Wash mushrooms and soak overnight or for several hours. Drain, saving liquid. Put all the vegetables except the tomatoes and mushrooms through a food chopper separately. Wash and salt the meat. Place meat, barley, tomatoes, and onions in the water; cook slowly for 1 hour. Add carrots, mushroom liquid, and mushrooms; cook another hour. Add celery and pepper; simmer half an hour. Add extra water, if too thick. Salt and pepper soup to taste while cooking. Serves 6.

MUSHROOM BISQUE

2 tbsp. butter
2 tbsp. minced onion
2 tbsp. minced green pepper
½ cup minced celery
1½ cups minced mushrooms
1 cup cream

1½ qt. soup stock
   or bouillon
Salt and pepper to taste
½ tsp. sugar
Few grains mace
⅓ cup cracker crumbs

Melt butter. Add minced vegetables. Cook for 5 minutes. Add stock and seasonings. Cook until celery is tender. Add the cracker crumbs and cream. Serves 8.

CONSOMME MADRILENE

Reduce 2 cups tomato purée over high heat to half its original volume, and add it to 1 quart hot chicken consommé. If necessary, a little beet juice may be added to intensify the color of the consommé if the tomato is not red enough. Makes 1 quart.

JELLIED MADRILENE

If the madrilene is to be served jellied, stir in 1 envelope gelatin softened in the beet juice. Cool the madrilene and chill until the gelatin sets.

CHILLED SPINACH SOUP

2 lb. sour cream
½ gallon water
4 chicken cubes
1 tsp. nutmeg

½ tsp. white pepper
1 lb. chopped spinach, drained
1 qt. half & half cream

Mix all ingredients in food processor. Chill overnight.

SPLIT PEA SOUP

1 lb. green split peas
1 clove garlic
1¼ gallons water
2 oz. margarine
2 lb. ham with fat

1 medium carrot, chopped
½ medium onion, chopped
1½ tsp. salt
1 tsp. pepper

In a large pot cook margarine and ham with fat for 8-10 minutes. Add onion, carrots, split peas, salt, pepper, garlic, and water. Let come to a boil, reduce to simmer, and cook for 1 hour and 45 minutes. Remove and strain through a fine strainer. Serves 10-12.

CHILLED GAZPACHO SOUP

24-oz. can tomato juice
3 large ripe tomatoes
2 large cucumbers
¼ cup tarragon vinegar
2 tsp. sugar
3 oz. pitted black olives
2 oz. Tabasco sauce

24-oz. can V-8 juice
¼ large bell pepper
¼ yellow onion
¼ cup salad oil
1 tsp. salt
1 tsp. white pepper

In blender place onion, bell pepper, cucumbers, salad oil, and tomato juice. Blend for 1-2 minutes and add the remaining ingredients. Blend for another 2-3 minutes. Place the soup in refrigerator to chill for 4 hours. Garnish with sour cream on top and serve. Makes 18 cups.

VICHYSSOISE
(Cold Cream of Potato and Leek Soup)

6 leeks, white parts only
2 tbsp. sweet butter
4 cups chicken broth
2 cups scalded milk
White pepper

2 small onions
5 potatoes
1 tsp. salt
1 cup cream

Slice the leeks and onions thin and cook them slowly in the butter for 10-15 minutes, stirring occasionally with a wooden spoon until they are soft but not browned. Add the chicken broth and the potatoes, diced, and cook for 15 minutes longer.

Add the scalded milk and bring the soup to boiling point. Season well with salt and white pepper and put the soup through a fine sieve or purée it in an electric blender. Chill thoroughly, add the cream, and serve in chilled cups with a sprinkling of chopped chives on each portion. Serves 8.

HOMEMADE VEGETABLE SOUP

This vegetable soup was served every Tuesday and Saturday at the Pontchartrain for over eighteen years. It has proven to be one of my best soups. People would come to get it by the gallons to take home with them. Makes 1 gallon.

1 cup diced tomatoes
4 oz. spaghetti, broken
  in small pieces
½ small cabbage, diced
2 ribs celery, diced
½ lb. veal shank, cut
  in small pieces
1½ lb. whole green beans
2 bay leaves
1½ oz. green peas

1 cup tomato sauce
½ medium yellow onion,
  diced
2 medium carrots, diced
1 cup corn
1 tsp. salt
¼ tsp. white pepper
½ gallon water
2 medium short ribs with
  bones

In a 1-gallon pot, heat ½ gallon water (cold), short ribs with bone, and veal shank with bone. Bring to a boil. Reduce heat and simmer for 45 minutes. Add onion and celery; cook for 15 minutes. Add tomato sauce, diced tomatoes, white pepper, salt, carrots, corn, green beans, green peas, bay leaves, and cabbage. Cook for 20 minutes, then add the broken spaghetti. Cook for 10 minutes and serve.

CREAM OF BROCCOLI SOUP

8 cups chicken stock
1 bay leaf
1 tsp. thyme leaves
2 cups heavy cream
½ medium yellow onion,
  chopped

1 rib celery, chopped
4 tbsp. butter
1 tbsp. flour
1 tbsp. salt
1 tsp. pepper
2 bunches broccoli

In pot, put the stem of the broccoli (reserve the bud) with stock. Cook for 20 minutes, remove, and strain. Save the stock in another pot. Put butter to melt with onion and celery, then cook 5 minutes longer. Add flour and mix well (do not brown). Add the stock from the broccoli, cream, salt, pepper, thyme, bay leaf, broccoli, and bud. Cook for 8 minutes and serve. Serves 6-8.

CHICKEN SOUP WITH ANGEL HAIR PASTA

I call this my "Get Well Soup" because every time my first restaurant employer Mr. Sclafani was not feeling well, he would tell me to fix him some chicken soup. It always worked!

14 oz. veal shanks, cut up
  with bone
10 cups cold water
5 oz. angel hair pasta, broken
½ tsp. salt
1 rib celery, chopped

1½ lb fryer, cut up
1 medium carrot, diced
1 bunch green onions
2 bay leaves
White pepper

In medium pot, put cold water. Add veal shanks, cut up, and chicken. Cook on low heat for 40 minutes, then add celery, carrots, bay leaves, pepper, and salt. Cook for 15 minutes more, and add green onions and broken pasta. Mix well, cook 10 minutes more, and let set. Skim off fat and serve. Makes 1½ gallons.

Salads and Vegetables

You can be very creative with salads and vegetables. Working as a chef, I have to come up with different salads, since many people like to eat just salad at lunchtime. There's one salad I created that combines pasta, crawfish, and crabmeat. It was created for a later lunch at the Pontchartrain Hotel. You can also use it for an appetizer. Crabmeat in New Orleans is on just about every menu. In the summer, crabmeat is plentiful. In the fall or when it gets cold, the crabs don't eat so they are not fat. The price goes up usually in January and February when the crabmeat is scarce.

Instead, you can use artichokes and more fresh vegetables in your salads. For example, there's an artichoke salad I use at Kabby's called Crabmeat Biarritz. You garnish with fresh vegetables and stuff it with crabmeat.

One tip for having crispy salad is, do not cut the lettuce with a knife. Break and wash it, then drain in a cloth and put in the freezer until ready for use.

Fresh vegetables play a great part in our lives. I like to use squash, eggplant, okra, corn, tomatoes, and artichokes. In this book, you will find that I have stuffed tomatoes with corn.

Squash are good vegetables. Take zucchini. It's better to sauté than undercook—it gets soft faster than yellow squash. Yellow squash is better for baking. Now that acorn squash is plentiful, you can stuff it, bake it, or use it for garnish. Also, there's butternut squash, which is sweeter than the others. I found many uses for it. And don't forget our Louisiana yams!

CRABMEAT BIARRITZ

This is a salad I have used for years. It can be used for lunch or as an appetizer. If crabmeat is out of season, you can use shrimp or crawfish. The only difference is that the shrimp won't hold together like the crabmeat. Also, when you cook the artichoke, make sure it is firm because you use the leaves to put the crabmeat in. I know you will enjoy this dish.

3 heads Boston lettuce
6 fresh artichokes, boiled
3 tomatoes, sliced
3 tsp. whole capers
1 tsp. black caviar
½ tsp. salt
¼ tsp. cayenne pepper

2 lb. crabmeat
1 rib celery, finely chopped
1¼ cups mayonnaise
½ cup whipping cream
  (whipped)
2 tsp. chives
French dressing

Clean artichoke, break off leaves, and set on side. Save the heart and soak in French dressing with the sliced tomatoes. On 6 plates, cover with the leaves of the Boston lettuce, then take the artichoke leaves and place one by one around the center of the plate. Put the sliced tomatoes in the center and put the heart of the artichoke on top of the tomatoes.

Put the crabmeat in a bowl. Add chopped celery, chopped chives, pepper, salt, and 1 cup mayonnaise. Mix together, then mold with demicup. Place on top of the artichoke.

Mix whipped cream and ¼ cup mayonnaise together and put about 2 oz. on top of each dish. Put the capers and caviar on top. Serve with French dressing. Serves 6. This is one of my most popular salads.

CRABMEAT AND CRAWFISH PASTA SALAD

I created this pasta salad at the time when pasta was on just about every restaurant menu. I used this salad for lunch, and it came to be one of my most famous salads (at the Pontchartrain). I featured a special salad at lunchtime everyday. I used mixed noodles to give it color. You can do so much with fresh crabmeat and crawfish. I was trained to use fresh ingredients and I have continued this tradition over the years.

½ lb. mixed pasta (cooked)
1 tsp. salt
1 tsp. thyme leaves
½ cup mayonnaise
¼ cup lemon juice
1 oz. green pepper sauce
½ lb. lump crabmeat
1 cup French dressing
    (see below)

¼ red bell pepper,
    finely chopped
¼ tsp. dill
1 tsp. garlic powder
1 tsp. cayenne pepper
½ cup chopped parsley
½ lb. crawfish tails

Mix herbs, mayonnaise, French dressing, lemon juice, pepper, salt, and garlic. Mix well and pour over pasta. Add crabmeat and crawfish tails, green pepper sauce, and bell pepper and mix well. Let sit in freezer for 2 hours. Serve on plate of Boston lettuce and garnish with tomato wedges, cucumber slices, and boiled egg. Serves 12.

FRENCH DRESSING

1 cup oil
¼ cup cider vinegar
½ tsp. sugar
1 tsp. salt

1 tsp. dry mustard
1 whole egg
¼ tsp. cayenne pepper

In blender, put cider vinegar, dry mustard, sugar, salt, and cayenne pepper. Put blender on slow. Add oil slowly and mix for 10 minutes, then add raw egg and chopped parsley.

CLINKEDAGGER'S SPINACH SALAD

¼ cup red wine vinegar
1 tsp. minced onion
½ tsp. Worcestershire sauce
¾ cup salad oil

1 tbsp. Dijon mustard
½ tsp. monosodium
  glutamate
Dash Tabasco sauce

Mix all ingredients and serve over salad below.

SALAD INGREDIENTS

5 cups (6 oz.) fresh spinach
½ cup sliced fresh
  mushrooms
1 tbsp. sliced almonds
  (cooked)
1 hard-boiled egg, coarsely
  chopped

1 tbsp. grated Romano
  cheese
8 leaves red-tip leaf lettuce
2 slices bacon, crisp-cooked
  and crumbled
½ cup croutons

Mix all salad ingredients together. Serves 6-8.

ENDIVE AND AVOCADO SALAD

Clean the endives and halve the stalks *lengthwise*. Arrange the endive halves on individual plates alternately with slices of avocado. Sprinkle with French dressing and a mixture of chopped chives and chervil.

SALAD ELISABETH

Clean the endive and halve the stalks *lengthwise*. Arrange the endive on plates and cover them with thin slices of cooked beets, mixed with French dressing. Sprinkle the salad with a mixture of chervil, tarragon, and chives, all finely chopped.

GREEN GODDESS SALAD

8 or 10 anchovy fillets
1 small onion
2 sprigs parsley
Fresh tarragon leaves
1 bunch fresh chives
3 cups mayonnaise

1 tbsp. tarragon vinegar
Salad greens (romaine,
   chicory, escarole)
Crab (optional)
Shrimp (optional)

Chop anchovy fillets with 1 small onion.

Chop parsley, a few fresh tarragon leaves (or preserved, if necessary), and chives. After these herbs are finely chopped, mash them together.

Combine the chopped anchovy fillets, chopped onion, and the mashed herbs with mayonnaise. Add tarragon vinegar. Mix this dressing with salad greens in a garlic-rubbed bowl. Serve immediately. Serves 8.

Note: Crab or small shrimp may be added to the salad.

GULF STAR SALAD

1 tsp. fennel seeds
½ cup olive oil
⅛ cup vinegar
1 cup vermouth (white)
1 tsp. garlic powder
½ tsp. cayenne pepper
½ tsp. basil

1 tsp. Dijon mustard
2 tsp. English-style
   horseradish
1 tsp. jalapeno pepper sauce
3 large Creole tomatoes,
   peeled and diced
½ tsp. Worcestershire sauce

Place all above in blender. Blend on slow speed 8-10 minutes. Set in refrigerator for 2 hours.

½ lb. Rotelle Pasta cook
   mix, cooked
3 large sliced mushrooms
1 rib sliced celery
1 medium diced red pepper
2 large Creole tomatoes,
   cut in wedges
½ tsp. basil
1 tsp. cayenne pepper
6 oz. trout, cut in small
   pieces

6 oz. flounder, cut in small
   pieces
6 oz. halibut, cut in small
   pieces
6 oz. lemon fish
2 bay leaves
2 cups vermouth (white)
2 medium lemons, cut in
   wedges
Onion flower

Place all the fish in flat pan. Pour vermouth over fish. Add bay leaves, cayenne pepper, lemon, and basil. Cook for 5 minutes. Turn heat off. Let cool. Drain. Put the pasta mix, sliced mushrooms, celery, and diced red pepper in a bowl. Mix lightly. Pour a small amount of dressing over it. Place leaves of radicchio on a plate. Garnish with Creole tomato wedges and onion flower. Serve and enjoy. Serves 6.

MAURICE SALAD BOWL

2 cups mayonnaise
¼ cup light cream
2 tbsp. lemon juice
1 tbsp. wine vinegar
1 tsp. each dry mustard
    and salt
½ tsp. monosodium
    glutamate

2 tbsp. chopped chives
3 hard-boiled eggs, coarsely
    chopped
1 medium dill pickle,
    chopped

Combine the ingredients in the order listed. Mix well. Arrange chunks of head lettuce in a salad bowl, top with thin julienne strips of cooked chicken and ham, and pour the dressing over the salad. Garnish with tomato wedges.

SALAD A LA GRECQUE

1 cup red wine vinegar
1 cup dry white wine
8 pitted green olives, not
    stuffed
12 Greek olives
1 tsp. chopped fresh
    tarragon
12 large, peeled, whole
    garlic cloves
6 2" pieces green onion
1 lemon flower, parsleyed
    and sprinkled with paprika

1 cup olive oil
2-3 oz. Shitake black
    mushrooms, quartered
6 large, peeled, whole
    shallots
¼ tsp. salt
Lettuce cup
1 Greek olive
Carrot slivers

In a frying pan, reduce the vinegar, oil, and wine until it is one-half the original amount and caramel colored. Add the mushrooms, green olives, the 12 Greek olives, garlic, shallots, tarragon, and salt to remaining liquid and simmer until only ½ cup of liquid remains. Allow mixture to cool.

To serve, spoon into lettuce cup and garnish with green onions, parsley, and lemon flower. Place Greek olive in center of lemon and scatter carrot slivers over top of salad. Makes 1 salad or 2 appetizers.

Note: For 2 appetizers you will need 2 lemon flowers and 2 Greek olives for garnish.

MARINATED AVOCADO-MUSHROOM SALAD

1 medium avocado, seeded, peeled and sliced
2 thin slices onion, separated in rings
2 tbsp. vinegar
1 cup sliced fresh mushrooms

¼ tsp. salt
¼ cup salad oil
¼ cup dry white wine
½ tsp. sugar
¼ tsp. dried basil
Crushed Bibb lettuce leaves

In bowl, combine avocado, mushrooms, and onion rings. In screw-top jar, combine oil, wine, vinegar, sugar, salt, and basil; shake well. Pour over vegetables. Cover and chill for 2-3 hours, stirring occasionally. Drain avocado mixture. Serve on lettuce leaves. Serves 4.

MADAME KUONY'S WALNUT OIL SALAD

Bibb lettuce, cleaned and
crisped
Belgian endive, cleaned and
crisped
3 tbsp. fine French walnut
oil

1½ tbsp. mild champagne
vinegar
Salt and pepper to taste
Chopped watercress for
garnish

Tear large lettuce leaves into bite-size pieces, leaving small inner leaves whole. Cut endive into bite-size pieces. Combine lettuce and endive in salad bowl. Beat walnut oil, vinegar, salt, and pepper with a wooden fork until the mixture looks opaque, then pour over greens and toss well. Sprinkle watercress on top. Serves 4.

SALAD NIÇOISE
(Olive and Anchovy Salad)

1 large tomato
½ lb. fresh string beans
8 ripe olives
1 medium onion
3 tbsp. olive oil
Salt and pepper

2 green peppers
5 oz. anchovies
3 eggs
1 medium can tuna fish
1 tbsp. wine vinegar

Wash and clean the beans and cook them for 20 minutes in rapid boiling, salted water. When tender, drain and cool. Hard-boil the eggs, then hold for an instant under cool running water. Peel and quarter 2 of them, cut the third in slices. Wash the peppers, remove seeds and filaments, and cut into small strips. Peel and slice the onion; slice the tomatoes; stone the olives. Hold the anchovies under cold running water for 10 minutes to remove excess salt. Drain.

Pile the vegetables, quartered eggs, anchovies, and the tuna in small chunks into a salad bowl. Pour over an oil and vinegar dressing seasoned with pepper and salt. Toss lightly, decorate with slices of egg, and serve.

Note: To keep beans green, put them bit by bit into the boiling pot so that the water never stops boiling. Do not cover. Serves 4-5.

PINEAPPLE CHICKEN SALAD A LA CHEF LOUIS EVANS, JR.

4 qt. chicken cooked and
  cubed
3 qt. celery, sliced
1½ qt. mayonnaise
1 tsp. white pepper
2 tsp. onion juice

Romaine lettuce, as needed
1 cup thin French dressing
3 cups green pepper, diced
4 tsp. salt
4 tsp. lemon juice
2 #10 cans pineapple slices

Marinate chicken in French dressing 1-2 hours. Mix celery, green pepper, mayonnaise, salt, pepper, and onion and lemon juices. For each serving, scoop ½-⅓ cup salad into bowl lined with leaves of romaine. Arrange 2 pineapple slices cut in half around salad. Garnish with carrot curls, ripe olives, green pepper rings and diced almonds as desired. Serve with dressing of crushed pineapple mixed with mayonnaise and sour cream. Makes about 2½ gallons salad or 50 5-oz. servings.

YAM SOUFFLE

Louisiana yams are still the best vegetable that we have. Yams can be used many ways as a vegetable or dessert. They make a mean sweet potato pie. You can buy them almost year round. I use them at Kabby's for a vegetable. Sometimes I just peel, slice, and bake them with brown sugar, butter, and cinnamon. But I prefer to peel and boil them, add butter, mace, cinnamon, cornstarch, cream, sugar, and egg, then put them in a flat pan, bake, and serve. Another great way to serve them is in this delicious soufflé.

2 lb. fresh Louisiana yams,
sliced ⅛" thick
1½ tsp. mace
2 tbsp. cornstarch
1 cup half & half
½ lb. margarine

4 cups water
½ tsp. nutmeg
2 whole eggs
1 tsp. orange zest, chopped
1¼ cups sugar

Cook yams in water for 25 minutes with ¼ cup of sugar and ¼ lb. margarine. Then drain. Put the cooked yams in blender. Add mace, nutmeg, half & half, remainder of sugar, margarine, orange zest, whole eggs, and cornstarch. Put in blender on medium. Blend 2-3 minutes. Then pour the mix in a 9-inch baking dish, and cook in 350° oven for 40 minutes. Serve and enjoy. Serves 6-8.

STUFFED EGGPLANT

Creole people have stuffed eggplant for years, before I was taught. It can be with ham, shrimp, or both—sometimes with crawfish and crabmeat. More restaurants today use stuffed eggplant as a main course. You will notice in my cookbook that it's in the old-fashioned style. For instance, I use soaked French bread. I was taught not to waste food. We always had left over French bread, and if we didn't use it to make bread pudding, we used it in stuffing.

Tip: When using eggplant, wash the chopping board and knife after use because they can be bitter and will have a tendency to spoil everything.

2 medium eggplants	1 lb. shrimp
1 medium white onion	1 small piece chopped ham
½ bunch green onions	2 eggs
Bacon drippings	½ tsp. sugar
2 tbsp. minced parsley	Salt and pepper to taste
3 to 4 small French loaves,	Dash thyme
soaked in water	Bread crumbs

Boil eggplants until tender. Let cool. Chop onion and the green onions finely. Sauté in bacon drippings. Do not brown. Then add shrimp and ham. Scoop out eggplant pulp carefully so as not to damage skin, then add pulp to the onion mixture. Simmer for 20 minutes and then remove from heat. Add the eggs, soaked bread, and mix well. Add salt, pepper, thyme, parsley, and sugar.

Put the mix in eggplant shell and sprinkle with bread crumbs. Bake in oven for about 20 minutes. Oven should be preheated to 375°. Serves 4.

STUFFED ACORN SQUASH

3 medium acorn squash
  (cooked)
1 tsp. thyme leaves
1 tsp. basil leaves
2 oz. green pepper sauce
1 tbsp. salt
½ cup chicken stock
1 medium bunch green
  onions, chopped
¼ lb. margarine

1 lb. crawfish tails
2 bay leaves
1½ cups bread crumbs
2 cloves garlic, chopped
½ tsp. cayenne pepper
¼ medium yellow onion,
  finely chopped
1 rib celery, finely chopped
2 tbsp. olive oil

Once the acorn squash is boiled, cut in half and take the seed out. Take a large spoon and scoop out the inside down to the hull, and chop it and set the hull aside for stuffing. In a saucepan, put the olive oil, chopped garlic, celery, green onions, and yellow onions together and cook for 8 minutes.

Add the chopped squash, chicken stock, bay leaves, thyme, basil, salt, cayenne pepper, green pepper sauce, and crawfish tails. Mix well. Let cook on low heat for 5-10 minutes, then add ½ cup bread crumbs, mix in, and stuff the squash hull. Sprinkle bread crumbs on top of each one. Melt the margarine and take a brush and sprinkle over each one. Bake in a preheated oven at 375° for 45 minutes and serve. Serves 6.

BAKED STUFFED POTATOES

Bake 3 large Idaho potatoes until they are tender. Cut the potatoes in half lengthwise and scoop out the pulp, leaving the shell intact.

In a pot, heat 1 pint of milk. Add the potato pulp to the milk, along with 2 oz. cheese, 2 oz. sour cream, ½ tsp. salt, and 2 tbsp. butter. Mix well. Place this mix into the potato shells. Sprinkle lightly with grated cheese and butter and bake in 375° oven for 15 minutes. Serve.

BUTTERNUT SQUASH

3 medium butternut squash
¾ lb. butter, melted
2 tsp. ground cinnamon
½ cup chopped pecans

1 lb. brown sugar
1 qt. pineapple juice
3 oz. coconut

Boil the squash until you can cut it in half. Take the seed and lay the squash flat on a chopping board. Slice it about ⅛ inch thick. Put in a flat baking pan, sprinkle with butter, cinnamon, and brown sugar, and pour in the pineapple juice and pecans. Bake in preheated oven at 375° for 35-45 minutes. Take the coconut and put in a flat pan. Put in the oven, let it toast to a light brown color, and sprinkle over the squash. Serve.

Note: Do not peel the squash. Serves 4.

IDAHO POTATOES LOUIS

½ strip bacon
¼ lb. butter
1 carrot, peeled and sliced
  ⅛" thick
1 medium zucchini squash,
  sliced ⅛" thick
1 Idaho potato, peeled and
  sliced ⅛" thick

Salt
White pepper to taste
1 cup water
¼ tsp. sugar
½ tsp. parsley, finely
  chopped

In sauté pan, add ¼ tsp. bacon grease, ¼ lb. butter, carrot slices, potato slices, 1 cup water, and cook for 15 minutes. Add zucchini squash, pepper, sugar, and salt. Cover and cook for 8-10 minutes more. Add chopped parsley and serve with a beef entree. Serves 2.

IDAHO POTATOES DAUPHINE

6 medium potatoes, peeled   1 pt. hot milk
   and diced small   8 egg yolks
Salt and pepper   1 cup chopped parsley
8 cups bread crumbs   4 cups all-purpose flour
½ tsp. nutmeg   1 pt. milk and 2 eggs,
½ lb. butter   beaten together

In pot, boil the diced potatoes for 20 minutes. Drain, then return to pot. Add butter, hot milk, salt, pepper, nutmeg, and egg yolks. Mix well and place in refrigerator for 1½ hours or until cold. When cold, roll potato mixture into golf-ball-size balls; roll the balls in 2 cups flour. Mix bread crumbs, remaining 2 cups flour, and 1 cup chopped parsley. Place potato balls in beaten milk and egg mixture, then the bread crumb mix, and fry in hot shortening (enough to cover potatoes) until brown. Serve with Trout Veronique. Serves 6-8.

IDAHO POTATOES DUCHESSE

6 medium potatoes   1 pt. hot milk
Salt and pepper   ½ lb. butter
6 egg yolks   1 tsp. yellow food coloring
1 tsp. nutmeg

Peel potatoes; cut into small pieces. Boil with salt and pepper until soft enough to mash. Drain and return to pan to dry. With a wire whisk, mash well, then add the hot milk, nutmeg, yellow food coloring, butter, egg yolks, and mix well. Place in a pastry bag and squeeze into little mounds on a flat greased pan. Bake in oven at 375° for 10 minutes and serve. Serves 6-8.

IDAHO POTATOES PARISIENS

Peel 6 to 8 medium Idaho potatoes; scoop out into little balls. Parboil balls for 5 minutes and drain. Heat 4 tbsp. butter in a shallow pan, add the potatoes, and cook on top of stove or in a hot oven (400°) until they are golden brown, stirring occasionally with a spatula without crushing them. Season with salt and pepper and sprinkle with finely chopped parsley. Serve with Trout Eugene. Serves 5-6.

RICE PILAU

3 tbsp. butter
2 cups rice
4 cups hot chicken broth (or water)

4 tbsp. finely chopped onions
½ tsp. salt
Melted butter

Melt butter in a saucepan that has a close-fitting cover. Add onion and rice, and roll all together over low heat for 2 minutes. Add broth (or water) and salt, cover closely, and bake in hot oven (400°) for 20 minutes. Remove from heat and turn rice into a hot serving dish. Add a little melted butter, tossing it in with a fork to prevent the grains from lumping. Serves 6.

STUFFED TOMATOES

6 whole tomatoes
1 oz. cream sauce
1 lb. cooked spinach, chopped

½ tsp. white pepper
1 tsp. salt

Mix chopped spinach with cream sauce. Add salt and pepper. Slice the bottom off the tomatoes. Take soup spoon and scoop out a hole in the tomato. Stuff with creamed spinach. Bake at 350° for 15 minutes. Serves 6.

STUFFED TOMATOES WITH CREOLE CORN

12 tomatoes
1 lb. cut corn
3 oz. chopped ham
¼ lb. butter
¼ bell pepper, finely
  chopped

¼ white onion, finely
  chopped
½ tsp. salt
¼ tsp. pepper
⅛ tsp. ground thyme

Cut about ⅛ off tops of tomatoes. Spoon out insides of each. Set aside. In sauté pan add butter, onion, ham, and bell pepper and sauté for 15 minutes. Add corn, thyme, salt, and pepper and cook for another 15-20 minutes, or until corn is tender. Fill tomatoes with mixture and bake in 350° oven for 15 minutes and serve.

EGGS ORIENTAL

1 cup sliced fresh
  mushrooms
¼ cup butter or margarine
1 can condensed cream of
  mushroom soup
½ cup grated American
  cheese

4 hard-boiled eggs, sliced
⅓ cup chopped green
  pepper
⅓ cup catsup
2 tbsp. milk
½ tsp. Worcestershire sauce

Sauté mushrooms and green pepper in butter until tender. Add soup and remaining ingredients except eggs. Heat, stirring, until cheese melts; add eggs. Serve over hot chow mein noodles or rice. Serves 4-5.

STUFFED MIRLITON

"Mil c tonu"

12 large mirlitons
½ bunch green onions
½ white onion
1 stalk celery
⅛ lb. ham
⅛ lb. butter

½ doz. shrimp
2 bay leaves
1½ cups bread crumbs
⅛ tsp. thyme
Salt and pepper to taste

Boil mirlitons until soft; cut in half. Scoop out insides and place in pan. In another pan, sauté the onion, celery, green onions, butter, ham, and shrimp until tender. Add mirliton pulp and cook for 20 minutes. Add salt, thyme, pepper, bay leaves, 1 cup bread crumbs, and mix together. Stuff mirlitons with mixture and sprinkle with rest of bread crumbs. Bake at 375° for 20 minutes and serve. Serves 12.

GRILLED MUSHROOMS

1½ doz. large mushroom
  caps
¼ tsp. salt
Dash nutmeg

¼ cup olive oil
Dash cayenne
¼ cup melted butter

Remove stems. Place caps in a deep dish. Pour olive oil over them; mix well. Let stand for 30 minutes. Remove from oil. Broil for about 8 minutes. Sprinkle with salt, cayenne, and nutmeg. Spoon melted butter over mushrooms. Serves 6.

ANGEL HAIR PASTA WITH GARLIC AND OIL

1 lb. angel hair pasta
4 tbsp. olive oil
2 tbsp. butter
4 cloves garlic, minced

Salt
Freshly ground black pepper
    or hot pepper flakes
1 bunch green onions, diced

Sauté green onions, garlic, and pepper in oil and butter over low heat until garlic is a very light brown. Meanwhile, cook angel hair pasta until al dente. Drain pasta well and add to sauté pan. Turn off heat and toss well. Season to taste. Serve immediately. Serves 4-6.

Sauces and Dressings

The key to a good restaurant is having good sauces and dressing. I was once told that the first thing you should do is train yourself a good sauce cook, a sauté cook, and someone to make your dressing. I find I was given good advice.

Most sauces should be served on the side, because some people like just a little. To make a delicious sauce you need good stock and time. Stock can be made two days ahead of time and put in the freezer. To make a good beef stock, go to the market and get a good bone. Wash, brown it in the oven, sprinkle flour on the bone so browning can be smooth, and add onion, celery bottoms, and carrots. Add water, 1-2 bay leaves, reduce by half, and strain until used. If you want chicken stock, boil the chicken first, then add a little onion and celery.

I believe Marchand du Vin Sauce is one of your class A sauces. Of course, red wine makes the difference. Be sure to let the wine cook out.

A lot of restaurants use a creamy dressing, more of a ranch type. I have a French dressing that I have used for years. This dressing can be a marinade for vegetables, fish, or chicken.

ROCKEFELLER SAUCE

1 tsp. cayenne pepper
½ bunch green onions,
  chopped
1 pint oysters
¾ cup herbsaint
1½ tbsp. thyme leaves
½ cup bread crumbs
3 bay leaves

2 ribs celery, chopped
½ medium yellow onion,
  chopped
2 lb. chopped spinach
2 tsp. anchovy paste
2 cloves garlic
1 tsp. salt

Grind all the above except the herbsaint, bread crumbs, and bay leaves. Blend in blender until chopped fine. Then place in pot with the herbsaint, bread crumbs, and bay leaves. Cook for ½ hour. Serves 6.

PARSLEY SAUCE

6 tbsp. coarsely chopped
  parsley
½ cup hot water
2 cups velouté sauce

Salt and white pepper to
  taste
¼ cup heavy cream

Blanch 5 tablespoons of the parsley in hot water. Cover and steep 5 minutes. Cool, strain, and dry in a clean towel. Add the 1 tablespoon remaining parsley to the velouté sauce. Bring to boiling point and simmer 3 to 4 minutes. Add dry blanched parsley and cream. Heat ½ minute. Season to taste with salt and pepper. Use with fish, egg, poultry, and vegetable dishes. Makes 2 cups.

MARCHAND DU VIN

If meat glaze is on hand, a tablespoon, melted, may be added to the butter. The butter may be prepared in advance but should not be semisoft and not chilled.

¾ cup good red wine
1 tbsp. finely chopped gray
    shallot (if unavailable,
    replace it with onion plus
    a small, finely chopped
    clove of garlic)

Salt to taste
Generous pinch of freshly
    ground pepper
6 oz. softened butter
1 tbsp. lemon juice
1 tbsp. chopped parsley

Reduce the wine and chopped shallot in a small saucepan over high heat to about ⅓ cup. Pour it in a mixing bowl and, when it is just tepid, whisk it vigorously with all the other ingredients.

PIQUANT SAUCE

This goes with leftover meats. Put into a saucepan 1 tablespoon vinegar, some salt and pepper, a little thyme, a bay leaf, and a little crushed hot red pepper. Cook until reduced to half, over moderate heat. Add 3 tablespoons of stock and reduce again until the sauce acquires the consistency of thin gruel. The "modern" method for preparing the same sauce is to season some chopped shallots with salt and pepper, put in saucepan with a 50-50 mixture of wine vinegar and white wine, and reduce over moderate heat. Moisten with stock, boil for 10 minutes, and then thicken with a little cornstarch over low heat. Just before serving add a little tarragon, parsley, chervil, pepper or paprika, and a few round slices of gherkin.

VOL-AU-VENT

Here is an uninvolved, delicious sauce, easy to make and flattering, as it should be, to the sophisticated, flaky container. Canned shrimp work beautifully.

5 tbsp. butter
7 oz. can button
  mushrooms, drained
1 tbsp. flour
1½ cups milk
1 cup light cream
1 tsp. salt
4 tbsp. flour
3 - 4½ oz. can shrimp,
  drained and rinsed

¼ tsp. white pepper
1 tsp. monosodium
  glutamate
2 egg yolks, slightly beaten
2 tbsp. diced pimento
1 tbsp. minced fresh parsley
¼ cup dry white wine

Melt butter in saucepan and sauté mushrooms until golden. Push mushrooms to one side of pan and blend in flour to make a roux. Add milk, cream, and dry ingredients. Cook and stir over low heat until mixture begins to thicken. Spoon a small amount of sauce into the egg yolks, then quickly stir eggs into sauce. Cook until thick and smooth, stirring constantly. Add pimento, parsley, wine, and shrimp; heat. Meanwhile, reheat pastry shell in 350° oven about 10-12 minutes. Remove pastry top from bottom of the shell; fill shell with sauce and replace top. Serve at once. Serves 6-8.

BROWN SAUCE

½ cup fat (fresh, unsalted
  beef, veal, or pork
  drippings but not chicken
  fat)
1 carrot, coarsely chopped
2 onions, coarsely chopped
½ cup flour
10 peppercorns
2 qt. Brown Stock, boiling

½ cup tomato sauce or ½
  cup tomato purée or juice
1 clove garlic, chopped
1 faggot made by tying
  together 2 stalks celery,
  3 sprigs parsley, a little
  thyme, and a small bay
  leaf

Melt fat in heavy saucepan. Add carrot, garlic, and onions and cook until they start to turn golden, shaking the pan so they will cook evenly. Add flour and cook, stirring frequently, until the flour takes on a good brown color (hazelnut brown) and the carrots and onions are also brown.

Add 3 cups of the boiling stock, pepper, and the faggot. Cook, stirring until the mixture thickens, and then add 3 more cups of stock. Cook very slowly, stirring occasionally until the mixture is reduced to about 3 cups (this should take about 1 to 1½ hours). As it cooks the excess fat will be constantly rising to the surface and should be skimmed off.

Add tomato sauce (or purée or juice) and cook a few minutes longer. Strain through a fine sieve. Add remaining 2 cups of stock and continue cooking slowly until the sauce is reduced to about 4 cups (this should take about 1 hour).

BROWN STOCK

1 to 2 lb. beef bones
1 to 2 lb. veal bones
1 carrot, sliced
½ tbsp. salt
2 onions, sliced

2½ qt. water
A faggot made by tying
    together 2 stalks celery,
    4 sprigs parsley, a little
    thyme, and a bay leaf

Spread bones in a shallow roasting pan, strew carrots and onions over, place in a moderately hot oven of 400°, and let cook until they are a very rich dark brown. Transfer to soup kettle; add water, salt, and faggot; and bring slowly to the boil, skimming when necessary. Continue cooking slowly for about 4 hours, when water should be reduced to about 2 quarts. Strain through a fine sieve or cheesecloth. Store in refrigerator until needed for making sauces which call for brown stock and for brown sauce. This stock can also be used to make French Onion Soup or Vegetable Soup. Makes 2 quarts.

WHITE BUTTER SAUCE

¼ cup white wine vinegar
¼ cup mixture white wine or
    dry vermouth and lemon
    juice (approximately 3
    tbsp. lemon juice balanced
    with white wine or
    vermouth to make ¼ cup)

1 tbsp. minced shallots
4 grinds of the peppermill
1 stick or more butter
1 tsp. salt

Cook the vinegar, lemon juice, and vermouth until it is reduced to approximately 2 tbsp. Then add the butter, approximately 1 tbsp. at a time, after putting the minced shallots in the wine/vermouth mixture. Add salt and pepper. Add butter continuously and stir with a wire whisk until the sauce is reduced to a syrupy consistency. This sauce is served over a mousseline of fish but I think it would be good on any fish. Makes 1 cup.

SWEET-SOUR SAUCE

¼ lb. dry apricots
1 cup water
½ cup granulated sugar
(more or less)

About ½ cup cider or other
vinegar (more or less)
¼ tsp. salt

Cook apricots in water in covered saucepan very slowly for about 30 minutes, or until very soft and most of the water has been absorbed by apricots. When soft, put apricots through food mill. Combine all ingredients and, with egg beater, beat until smooth and thoroughly blended. Taste and season further if necessary. Serve with Cantonese appetizers. May be made days in advance and stored in covered jar in refrigerator. Makes 1½ cups.

HOT SAUCE

½ cup cool water
About 1½ tbsp. dry mustard
(more or less, to suit taste)

About ¾ cup catsup
1 tsp. salt

Combine all ingredients and, with egg beater, beat until smooth and thoroughly blended. Serve with Cantonese appetizers. May be made days in advance and stored in covered jar in refrigerator. Makes 1 cup.

ROBERT SAUCE

Serve only with fresh pork. Fry a few chopped onions lightly in butter, moisten with a little stock, season with salt and pepper, and simmer for half-hour. Then, over a gentle heat, add a few drops of vinegar, a dash of powdered sugar, a little mustard, and chopped tarragon. Mix with a wire whisk and serve in a heated sauceboat or pour over the meat.

BORDELAISE SAUCE

2 tsp. finely chopped
  shallots
1 cup Brown Sauce (see
  index for recipe)

½ tsp. chopped parsley
1 glass (4 oz.) red wine
2 tbsp. beef marrow

Put shallots and wine in a saucepan and cook until reduced to about ¾ the original quantity. Add Brown Sauce and cook about 10 minutes. Just before serving add beef marrow which has been cut into small cubes and placed in lukewarm water for a few minutes and drained. Add parsley. (Use for steak.) Makes 1 cup.

BLACK BUTTER
(Beurre Noir)

½ cup butter
1 tbsp. chopped parsley

1 tsp. white wine vinegar
1 tbsp. capers

Cook butter in heavy saucepan over medium heat to a dark brown color and pour into a bowl. Add the vinegar to the hot pan; let it fizz. Add that to the butter. Mix in the capers and parsley, and stir well. Makes half a cup. Use for eggs, fish, boiled peas, or beans.

TARTAR SAUCE

¼ bunch green onions,
  finely chopped
4 dill pickles, finely chopped

2 tsp. lemon juice
1 qt. mayonnaise
¼ yellow onion, chopped

Mix all the ingredients together and chill. Makes 1½ quarts.

BECHAMEL SAUCE

4 tbsp. butter
½ cup flour
3 pt. boiling milk
5 white peppercorns
Pinch grated nutmeg
(optional)

2 tbsp. finely chopped
onion (optional)
½ tsp. salt
2 sprigs parsley

Melt butter in a saucepan, add onion, if used, and cook until it is soft but not brown. Add flour, mix well, and cook slowly until the flour just starts to turn golden. Add milk, a pint at a time, stirring vigorously, preferably with a wire whip. Add salt, peppercorns, parsley, and, if desired, the nutmeg.

Cook slowly, stirring frequently for about 30 minutes or until reduced to ⅔ the original quantity and the sauce is the consistency of a very heavy cream. Strain through a fine sieve. Makes 1 quart of Béchamel. The onion is omitted if the sauce is for very delicate foods or if the flavor is not liked. Use for vegetables, fish, poultry, or any "creamed" dish, and as the base for Mornay, Cream, and other sauces.

HOLLANDAISE SAUCE

8 egg yolks
1 lb. butter
1 oz. tarragon vinegar
1 cup crushed ice

1 oz. water
Dash Tabasco
Dash salt

Melt butter. Put eggs over a double boiler, and when butter is melted, add slowly to the eggs. Beat constantly. Add tarragon vinegar, water, salt, and Tabasco. Stir constantly until tight. Take off heat and add ice. Serves 8.

RAVIGOTE SAUCE

1 pt. mayonnaise
1 oz. anchovy paste
1 tsp. cayenne pepper
½ cup sherry
1 tsp. tarragon leaves

1 oz. green pepper, chopped
1 oz. red pepper, chopped
2 tsp. green pepper sauce
1 tsp. Worcestershire sauce
1 tsp. lemon juice

Mix all sauce ingredients well, then place in refrigerator for 2 hours and serve with potatoes. Serves 6.

CREOLE POTATOES

2 packets crab boil
2 dozen new potatoes
1 gallon water

4 lemons, cut in half
2 tbsp. cayenne pepper
1 tbsp. salt

Boil whole potatoes in other ingredients for 20-25 minutes. Let sit in same for 15 minutes. Drain potatoes and serve with Ravigote Sauce.

MUSTARD SAUCE

2 cups mayonnaise
6 oz. Creole mustard

6 oz. yellow mustard

Mix together. Serves 6-8.

TOMATO SAUCE

3 oz. olive oil
1 medium yellow onion,
  chopped
1 cup tomato paste
½ tsp. salt
¼ tsp. pepper
½ tsp. basil

2 cloves garlic, chopped
2 bay leaves
2 cups tomato sauce
7 cups water
½ tsp. oregano
½ tsp. brown sugar

Heat olive oil in pot; add chopped garlic and onion. Brown the onion and add tomato paste with sugar. Reduce heat. Let cook until paste starts to separate. Add tomato sauce, water, oregano, basil, bay leaves, salt, and pepper, mix well. Let simmer for about 1½ to 2 hours. Makes 4 cups.

RICH CHOCOLATE-BRANDY SAUCE

1 cup heavy cream
*4 oz. semisweet chocolate
½ tsp. vanilla

⅔ cup sugar
2 tbsp. brandy

Heat cream, sugar, and chocolate in small heavy saucepan over low heat, stirring gently until chocolate melts and mixture bubbles, about 3 minutes. Whisk vigorously until mixture is smooth and well blended. Heat to boiling; reduce heat to low. Boil gently, stirring frequently, about 5 minutes. Remove from heat; cool slightly. Stir in brandy and vanilla. Serve slightly warm or at room temperature. Makes about 1½ cups.

*Tip: Bittersweet and semisweet chocolate can be used interchangeably in this recipe. For best flavor, use a good-quality chocolate.

SIMPLE SABAYON SAUCE

4 egg yolks
⅓ cup dry Marsala wine

4 tbsp. sugar
¼ tsp. vanilla extract

Put all ingredients into a deep saucepan or double boiler top (not aluminum) and beat with a wire whip. Place over boiling water and beat constantly until mixture thickens a little and becomes foamy. Serve hot. Serve in coupe glass over 6 or 7 well-hulled strawberries. Pass extra sauce at table. Makes 1 cup.

THE PONTCHARTRAIN'S RUM SAUCE

2 qt. milk
6 tsp. cornstarch
6 egg yolks
1 cup rum
2 tbsp. flour

1 cup sugar
Pinch salt
1 tsp. nutmeg
    (approximately)

Mix all ingredients together. Put in double boiler, stirring constantly until you obtain desired thickness. If a yellow color is desired, add yellow food coloring. Makes 2⅓ quarts.

FRUIT SALAD DRESSING

1 cup pineapple juice
Juice of 1 lemon
1 tbsp. prepared mustard
2 egg yolks, beaten

½ cup sugar
Dash salt
1 cup whipping cream,
    whipped

Combine all ingredients except whipped cream in a small saucepan. Cook over low heat, stirring occasionally, until smooth and thickened (about 30 minutes). Cool; fold in whipped cream just before serving. Serve over fruit. Makes about 2 cups.

FRENCH DRESSING

1½ tsp. sugar
1½ tsp. salt
1½ tsp. mustard
1½ tsp. black pepper

1½ tsp. cayenne pepper
¾ cup cider vinegar
3 cups salad oil
1 raw egg

In blender or food processor, on speed #1, mix salad oil and vinegar. Slowly add dry ingredients and mix for another 10 minutes after combined. Before serving beat in raw egg. Makes 1 quart.

POPPY-SEED DRESSING

This dressing is especially designed for fruit salads. Whenever possible use fresh fruits and be sure to have them thoroughly chilled.

1 cup sugar
2 tsp. salt
3 tbsp. onion juice
3 tbsp. poppy seeds

2 tbsp. dry mustard
⅔ cup vinegar
2 cups salad oil

Mix sugar, mustard, salt, and vinegar. Add onion juice and stir in thoroughly. Add oil slowly, beating constantly with an electric mixer or in a blender, and continue beating until thick. Add poppy seeds and beat a few minutes longer. Makes 3½ cups.

SOUR CREAM DRESSING #1

1 cup sour cream
1 tsp. lemon juice
Dash cayenne
¼ tsp. dry mustard

½ cup mayonnaise
1 tbsp. horseradish
Salt and paprika

Mix all together.

SOUR CREAM DRESSING #2

2 tbsp. vinegar
2 tbsp. sugar
Paprika

1 tsp. salt
1 tsp. mustard
1 cup thick sour cream

Add vinegar and seasonings to sour cream and pour over greens and vegetables.

CORN BREAD AND PECAN DRESSING

1 turkey neck
1 lb. creamed cornmeal
1 tsp. whole thyme leaf
1 tsp. rosemary
½ medium bell pepper, finely chopped
1 tsp. garlic, finely chopped
3 chicken wings
½ tsp. cayenne pepper
1 cup chopped pecans
2 tsp. chicken base
½ cup baking powder

6 giblets
½ bunch green onions, chopped
6 eggs
1 rib celery, finely chopped
¼ medium yellow onion, chopped
3 pork patties, finely chopped
½ tsp. black pepper
2 tsp. Worcestershire sauce

On slow heat, boil turkey neck and giblets in 3 quarts water. When water has reduced to 1 quart, turn off heat. Save the stock. In a pot, put the pork patties to cook. Then add garlic, pecans, green onions, onion, celery, and bell pepper. Cook for 10 minutes. Then add creamed cornmeal, cayenne pepper, Worcestershire sauce, eggs, rosemary, thyme, and black pepper. Mix well together. Add baking powder, turkey neck, wings, giblets, stock, and chicken base. Mix everything well. Place in baking dish. Set oven at 350°. Bake for 1 hour and 15 minutes. Makes 2 quarts.

OYSTER DRESSING

Oyster Dressing for Thanksgiving in New Orleans is a must. Corn Bread Dressing is also popular. I worked at the Pontchartrain Hotel for years and the people always wanted Oyster Dressing. We saw a lot of families eating out, but not anymore. Once the kids get past twelve years old it seems like the families stay away. I used to cook ten to fifteen small turkeys to be carved at the table (not anymore). This Oyster Dressing recipe was made with soaked French bread. Enjoy.

1 qt. drained oysters	1 oz. Worcestershire sauce
½ bunch green onions, finely chopped	½ white onion, finely chopped
3 pork patties	4 eggs
1 clove garlic, finely chopped	1 rib celery, finely chopped
1 French loaf, soaked and drained	1 dozen boiled, ground giblets
1 tbsp. chicken base	1 oz. jalapeno pepper sauce
1 tsp. cayenne pepper	1 tsp. sage
2 bay leaves	1½ tsp. thyme

In sauté pan, add pork patties. Mash until they look like ground meat. Cook for 5 minutes, then add garlic, celery, onions, and green onions. Cook for 8 more minutes.

Add whole oysters. Cook for 20-25 minutes. Add bay leaves, cayenne pepper, jalapeno pepper sauce, chicken base, thyme, ground chicken giblets, Worcestershire sauce, and sage. Mix well. Mix in the French loaf, that has been soaked and drained. Add eggs that have been beaten. Mix well.

Place in the oven at 350° for 1 hour. Remove. Serve and enjoy. Serves 8-10.

Meats

It seems that I have created fewer meat entrees than anything else. I guess I don't really like meat. But life goes on and I came up with some good recipes. Being a chef you cook what people want. When I worked for the late Peter Sclafani, he taught me how to make meatballs and spaghetti, from cutting the meat to grinding it. There's a difference when you learn where the meat comes from—the steaks, T-bones, fillets, lamb chops, shank legs, etc. We bought the whole lamb, and half a cow. When I see a steak or veal or whatever, I know what I'm looking at.

Mr. Sclafani taught me how he made Lasagna. We used ground meat, eggplant, and three cheeses. It turned out to be one of the best. I am not afraid to serve it to anyone.

Two of the most popular meats served in the coffee shop at the Pontchartrain were Pot Roast Jardinière, and Spicy Lamb Shanks. The coffee shop in the Pontchartrain served lunch and dinner. I would run a special, consisting of chicken, pork, seafood, beef, veal, and two vegetables. At Kabby's I use three cuts of meat: veal chops, porterhouses, and fillets. I serve more seafood but I still feature a starch, vegetable, and two specials a day.

BAKED LASAGNE

1 lb. dry flat lasagne noodles, boiled
2 medium eggplants, peeled, sliced, fried, and drained
1 cup cottage cheese
1½ cups grated cheese (Parmesan)
2 cups tomato paste
3 cloves garlic, chopped
1 tsp. basil
¼ cup olive oil
½ medium yellow onion, chopped
½ medium bell pepper, chopped
½ tsp. cinnamon
1 tsp. sugar
1 tbsp. salt
1 cup sour cream
2 bay leaves
24 oz. ground meat
1 cup tomato purée
1 lb. provolone cheese, sliced
1½ tsp. oregano
1 tsp. white pepper
3 cups water
1 tsp. Worcestershire sauce

Make the meat sauce. In saucepan, put olive oil, onion, garlic, bell pepper, ground meat, pepper, salt, basil, oregano, bay leaves, Worcestershire sauce, and cinnamon. Cook for 15 minutes. Add tomato paste, purée, water, and sugar. Let cook on low heat for 45 minutes.

In a baking dish place lasagne to cover the bottom of pan, put meat sauce, sprinkle grated cheese, cover with eggplant, and cover with provolone cheese. Then cover with Lasagne. Repeat until all of the eggplant, provolone cheese, and noodles are gone, then mix the sour cream and cottage cheese together and put all over the top with grated cheese. Bake in oven at 350° for 45 minutes to 1 hour. Serves 10-12.

STEAK AU POIVRE WITH RED WINE SAUCE

2½ lb. boneless sirloin steak
Salt
2 tbsp. peanut oil
2 tbsp. finely chopped
 shallots
2 tbsp. Cognac
1 tbsp. lemon juice

2 tbsp. coarsely ground
 black pepper
3 tbsp. butter
¾ cup red wine
1 cup brown sauce or
 canned beef gravy

Sprinkle the steak with salt to taste and rub in the pepper. Brown on all sides in the oil. Cook for 30-40 minutes, to the desired doneness. Transfer the steak to a warm serving platter and pour off the fat from the skillet. Add 1 tbsp. of the butter and all the shallots to the skillet.

Add the wine and stir to dissolve the brown particles on the bottom of the pan. Cook until the wine is reduced to ¼ cup. Add the Cognac, cook for 1 minute, and stir in the brown sauce. Remove the sauce from the heat, add the remaining butter, and swirl the pan until butter melts. Add lemon juice and serve with the sliced steak. Serves 4.

PRIME RIB DIABLO

I created this dish when I had a buffet every Sunday. I had prime rib on the buffet menu, which meant I had all of these end pieces of beef. So, I sliced it, made a mustard sauce, put it on the special, and the people liked it. The name *Diablo* came from the mustard A-1 Sauce with a pinch of brown sugar, which gives a sweet and sour taste.

Prime rib slice (⅛" - ½")
½ cup all-purpose flour
2 oz. yellow mustard
3 cups bread crumbs
3 oz. A-1 Sauce

½ cup water
¼ cup chopped parsley
6 oz. brown sugar
3 oz. Worcestershire sauce

Mix brown sugar, yellow mustard, A-1 Sauce, Worcestershire sauce, and water together in a bowl. Place the prime rib in this mixture. In another pan mix the bread crumbs, parsley, and flour together. Dust the prime rib slice in the bread crumbs and grill on low heat, brown on both sides, and serve. Serves 3-4.

TOURNEDOS HENRI IV

3½ lb. filleted beef
6 slices bacon
4 oz. salt pork
6 large mushroom caps
6 artichoke bottoms
6 rounds bread
2 cups shoestring potatoes

1 bunch watercress
2 oz. butter
1 small clove garlic
Salt
Pepper
Béarnaise Sauce

Cut the salt pork into thin strips. Thread into a larding needle and lard the fillet of beef. Rub with a cloth for ½ hour, and then cut into 6 slices. Put a little crushed pepper on the top of each, tie a slice of bacon around the outside of each, and season with garlic. Put a little butter on each tournedos and broil quickly on each side. Arrange on a round of fried bread on a hot, flat serving dish in the form of a circle. Then heat the artichoke bottoms in a little butter, salt, and pepper. Put a spoonful of Béarnaise Sauce in the center of each and cover with a sautéed mushroom cap. Fill the center of the serving dish with shoestring potatoes. Garnish with watercress. Serve the remaining sauce separately.

TOURNEDOS A LA BEARNAISE

4 tournedos
½ tsp. crushed garlic
Salt and pepper
4 rounds bread

5-6 tsp. butter
4 large mushroom caps
4 small mushroom caps

Season tournedos with garlic, salt, and pepper. Sauté in 2 tbsp. hot butter. Remove the tournedos and keep them warm. Melt another 2 tbsp. butter in the same pan and sauté 4 large and 4 small mushroom caps. Remove them. Again in the same pan fry 4 rounds of white bread which are slightly larger than the tournedos until golden brown on both sides, adding more butter as needed. Meanwhile, make the following Béarnaise Sauce.

BEARNAISE SAUCE

¼ cup vinegar
¼ cup white wine
1 tsp. chopped shallots or
    onions
Salt and peppercorns
Pinch thyme
Few drops lemon juice
2 large egg yolks

1 tbsp. cream
¼ lb. butter
1 tsp. chopped tarragon
½ tsp. chopped parsley
1 small bay leaf
Watercress or parsley for
    garnish

Put vinegar, dry white wine, finely chopped shallots or onions, a pinch of salt, 3-4 peppercorns, thyme, and a small crushed bay leaf into a small saucepan. Cook over gentle heat until reduced to 2 tbsp. Cool a little and strain into a small bowl. Add egg yolks and cream and beat until smooth with a small wire whisk. Put the bowl into a skillet with about an inch of simmering water in the bottom and beat over low heat until the mixture begins to thicken. Then beat in butter, bit by bit. Just before serving, add finely chopped tarragon, finely chopped parsley, and lemon juice.

Place the bread rounds on a hot serving dish and top with the tournedos. Put a large mushroom cap, stem side up, on each and fill the caps with Béarnaise Sauce, letting some sauce spill over and cover the meat. Top with the small mushroom caps; garnish with watercress or parsley and serve immediately. Serves 4.

TOURNEDOS SAUTES
(Sautéed Sliced Fillets)

Season 6 tournedos, cut less than 1½ inches thick, with salt and pepper. Heat enough clarified butter in a skillet to cover the bottom of the pan well. Arrange the pieces of meat side by side and brown them over high heat for 2-5 minutes on each side, depending on the thickness of the meat and the degree of doneness desired. Remove the meat to a serving dish.

Add ¼ to ½ cup stock or red wine to the pan and cook, stirring in all the brown bits, until the liquid is reduced by half. Swirl in 1 tbsp. butter and pour the sauce over the meat.

ENTRECOTE MARCHAND DU VIN
(Rib Steak with Red Wine Sauce)

2 or 3 rib steaks, 2" thick	1 tbsp. chopped shallots
1 tbsp. olive oil	2 cups red wine
1 tbsp. brown stock	2 tbsp. sweet butter
1 tsp. chopped parsley	Juice of ½ lemon

Allow about ½ pound boned weight for each serving. Spread the steaks with the olive oil and broil them to the rare stage. While the steaks are broiling, cook the red wine, stock, and shallots over high heat until the liquid is reduced to ½ cup. Stir in the butter, parsley, and lemon juice and add salt and freshly ground pepper to taste. Season the steaks with salt and remove them to a serving platter. Pour the sauce over the meat and carve the steaks at the table, in diagonal strips.

POT ROAST

This is a basic recipe and may be altered to suit personal taste by the addition of other spices, by substituting wine for the stock, or by using half wine and half stock. In a heavy cast-iron kettle put a piece of suet about the slice of an orange, flattened out. Add ½ cup each carrots, onions, leeks, parsley root, celery, and white turnips, all very closely chopped. Set the kettle on medium heat to brown the vegetables lightly.

After 5 minutes, turn the suet. When it is well rendered, lay a 5-lb. piece of beef, tied with butcher string, on the suet. Any cut of beef except shoulder, neck, or flank can be used to make pot roast. Raise the heat and sear the meat well on all sides, turning with a wooden spoon. Do not pierce it with a fork. Season with salt and freshly ground pepper to taste and add 8 whole peppercorns.

Pour over the beef enough scalded stock to cover and add a bouquet garni. Cover the kettle and set it in a moderate oven for 1¾ hours. Shake the pot at least three times during the braising to prevent the meat from sticking. Meanwhile, cook separately as many peas, carrots, and glazed onions as needed and keep them hot. Lift the roast from the kettle, place it on a platter, and keep it hot. Strain the gravy in the kettle through a medium sieve, forcing through as much of the vegetable pulp as possible. The resulting gravy should need no thickening. Reheat the vegetables in the gravy, slice the pot roast, and pour gravy and vegetables over all. Serves 6-8.

OLD-FASHIONED POT ROAST

1 6-7 lb. fresh brisket point
Salt, pepper, paprika, and
   flour
2 cups consommé, hot
1 cup hot water
2 large onions, diced

2 large carrots, sliced
1 bay leaf
1 #2½ can solid pack
   tomatoes
½ tsp. sugar

Rub brisket point with salt, pepper, paprika, and flour. Melt ½ cup vegetable shortening in a piping-hot, preheated Dutch oven or a large iron skillet on top of the stove. Put the meat in the fat and turn several times until it has a brown, appetizing look. This method seals in the juices. After searing process, discard fat.

Place onions and carrots around the meat. Add bay leaf, hot consommé, and hot water. Cover the pot and simmer on moderate heat for 4½ to 5 hours. The average piece of brisket point will take 5 hours before it is sufficiently tender. Under no circumstances should this delicious dish be rushed.

During the last hour add the tomatoes. Stir the tomatoes down into the liquid, and add sugar. (I have found that a touch of sugar used sparingly whenever tomatoes are called for helps remove their acid flavor and creates a smooth blend that is highly desirable.) Cover the pot again and continue to simmer until done. Serve with potato pancakes or with mashed potatoes and above all with the wonderful strained gravy.

Note: In this marvelous pot roast it is hard to say which is better, the meat or the gravy. To assure you of the best possible gravies, try this. Prepare the pot roast early in the day so that the gravy may be strained and allowed to rest in the kitchen in a mixing bowl. The fat will rise to the top and most of it can be removed and discarded. The defatted liquid is poured back into the pot, and at the appointed time the cooled meat is reheated in a delicious greaseless gravy. If you wish to thicken gravy it may interest you to know that the vegetables that have been cooked along with the meat need not be counted a total loss. They may be pressed through a sieve and added to the broth. This thickens the broth, adds to its flavor, and to your sense of thrift. Serves 8.

WHOLE ROASTED BEEF TENDERLOIN

Have a large fillet of beef trimmed and larded, ready for roasting. Rub with a cut clove of garlic. Place on a rack with drip pan underneath. Brush well with soft or melted butter. Sprinkle with salt and pepper. Roast fillet at 425° for 30 minutes, then reduce heat and continue to cook at 300° for about 20 minutes more per pound for rare, 25 minutes more per pound for medium, 30 minutes more per pound for well done. It is better to use a meat thermometer to determine doneness of meat, inserting it at one end of meat.

Baste meat every 15 minutes with melted butter or drippings in pan. Watch closely, and as soon as drippings appear in pan add 1 cup hot vegetable or meat stock to prevent scorching. Add more liquid as needed. Any leftover liquid and drippings in pan can be used for gravy. When meat is done remove to hot platter; let stand about 15 minutes before slicing and serving.

Meanwhile, prepare gravy with drippings in pan. Add more liquid to make desired amount of gravy. For each cup of liquid add 1½ tsp. (or more) cornstarch diluted in 2 tbsp. cool water (or 3 tbsp. flour diluted in ¼ cup water).

Cook until thick, then let simmer about 5 minutes, adding salt and other seasonings to taste. Pour some of the gravy over meat to serve. Garnish top of meat with large, sautéed, carved mushrooms (preferably with stems cut off).

POT ROAST JARDINIERE

I had a chance to work with the late James Beard. He and I did this recipe together at the Pontchartrain Hotel. He was a friend of the late Lysle Aschaffenburg. We spent a day together working on this dish. Afterwards, Mr. Lysle wanted me to have this pot roast served in the coffee shop every Saturday night, so I did for fifteen years, and we always sold out. James Beard asked me to do some demonstrations with him while he was in town the following week. I really enjoyed working with him.

6 lb. beef bottom rounds
1 cup all-purpose flour
½ cup tomato sauce
½ medium yellow onion, diced
1 tbsp. salt
½ tbsp. pepper
4 cups water

1 tbsp. thyme
4 bay leaves
2 carrots, diced
2 ribs celery, diced
½ cup oil
3 cloves garlic, chopped
1 cup red wine

In a heavy roasting pan, heat oil. Plug the roast with garlic, salt, and pepper. Dust with a little flour, then brown in shortening. Add remaining flour and cook until the flour is brown. Add celery, carrots, onion, and bay leaves. Cook for 15 minutes. Add tomato sauce, red wine, thyme, and water; stir and cover. Do not use foil. You don't want the roast to steam. Cook for 1 hour at 350°. Check to see if tender. Serves 10-12.

JELLIED BEEF TONGUE

1 fresh beef tongue
Water to cover
1 small onion, peeled and sliced
1 bay leaf
1 envelope unflavored gelatin
1¾ cups hot broth

Few drops red food coloring
1 tbsp. salt
4 black peppercorns
½ lemon
¼ cup cold water
¼ cup port wine

Place tongue in a large saucepan, cover with water, and add salt, onion, peppercorns, bay leaf, and lemon. Bring to a boil, cover, and simmer until tongue is tender. (It usually takes 1 to 1¼ hours to the pound.) Let tongue cool in the water until it can be handled. Cut off the bones and gristle from the thick end, slit skin down the center or underside, and peel off carefully. Strain the broth, measure out 1¾ cups, and season if necessary. Soak gelatin in cold water, then dissolve in hot broth. Add port wine and red food coloring. Chill until mixture is the thickness of unbeaten egg white, then spoon some of it over the tongue. Pour remaining gelatin mixture in a shallow pan and chill until firm. When ready to serve, slice the tongue and spoon the jellied mixture over the slices to garnish. Serves 4-5.

SALISBURY STEAK

4 strips bacon
1 tbsp. minced green pepper
1 tsp. salt
1½ lb. ground beef (chuck
   or round)

1 tbsp. chopped onion
1 tbsp. chopped parsley
½ tsp. pepper

Chop bacon and mix lightly with meat, onion, green pepper, parsley, and seasonings. Shape into cakes and place them 3 inches under broiler heat. Broil 12 minutes, turning once. Serves 6.

STEAK AU PINOT NOIR

2 individual boneless steaks,
   ½ lb. each
1 tbsp. olive oil
1 tbsp. white peppercorns

1 tsp. chopped shallots
½ cup Burgundy red
   (Pinot Noir)
Salt

Put the peppercorns in a cloth and pound them well with a hammer. Pat the crushed pepper into both sides of the steaks. Sprinkle the meat with oil and brown it rapidly on both sides under a hot broiler, or brown the steaks in the oil in a skillet. Simmer the shallots in a little butter, add the wine and a little salt, and cook for 2 minutes. Put the cooked steaks in this sauce for a minute, then remove them to the serving dish. Reduce the sauce over high heat until the moisture is almost entirely evaporated. Remove the pan from the stove and stir in 1 tbsp. sweet butter, bit by bit. Adjust the seasoning and pour the sauce over the steaks. Serves 2.

BEEF STEW WITH DUMPLINGS

1½ lb. lean beef top round,
  cup into 1½" cubes
1 cup tomato juice
2 cups thinly sliced onions
1 tbsp. chopped parsley
⅛ tsp. dried thyme leaves
2 medium carrots, sliced
  into 2" pieces

2 tsp. salt
Fluffy Dumplings
  (see below)
1 12-oz. can beer
1 clove garlic, finely
  chopped
1 bay leaf
⅛ tsp. pepper

Brush the bottom of a Dutch oven or heavy saucepan lightly with oil and heat over moderately high heat (about 350°); add some of the meat and brown on all sides. As meat browns, remove from pan. Continue until all the meat is browned. Add all meat back to pan. Reduce heat to low (about 200°).

Add tomato juice to pan. Add beer, onion, garlic, parsley, thyme, bay leaf, salt, and pepper. Cover and simmer 2 hours. Add carrots and continue cooking for 30 minutes. Remove from heat and cool. Cover and refrigerate overnight. The next day, remove all fat from surface of stew. Place over moderate heat (about 250°) and cook until stew comes to a boil. Spoon heaping tablespoonfuls of dumpling batter over stew, leaving about 1 inch between each dumpling. Cook uncovered, for 10 minutes. Then cover and cook 20 minutes, or until dumplings are cooked through and dumpling surfaces are dull. Serves 4-6.

FLUFFY DUMPLINGS

1⅔ cups sifted all-purpose
  flour
2 tsp. baking powder
⅛ tsp. ground thyme

¾ cup liquid skim milk
⅓ tsp. salt
1 egg white

Sift flour, baking powder, salt, and thyme into a bowl. Make a well in the center and add egg white and skim milk; stir well until flour is moistened. Drop heaping tablespoonfuls of batter onto stew, following directions above.

ROAST BEEF HASH, SOUTHERN STYLE

Roast Beef Hash is an old Southern dish. The old recipe I use is made with a thin brown gravy and you serve it with grits. Then the Creole people made it with a light Creole sauce and served it with rice. The cut of the meat should be chuck, diced in small pieces so it is bite-size. This recipe was created for the coffee shop at the Pontchartrain Hotel in New Orleans. I used to serve it every Monday as a Luncheon Special.

2 lb. top butt, diced in small pieces
2 ribs celery, chopped
½ bell pepper, chopped
3 oz. peanut oil
2 oz. flour
1 tbsp. thyme leaf
7 cups water
1 tsp. chopped garlic
1 yellow onion, chopped
4 bay leaves
½ tsp. salt
1 tsp. white pepper
2 medium Idaho potatoes, diced
1 oz. Worcestershire sauce

In heavy pot let peanut oil get hot, add diced beef, and let brown on both sides. Add garlic and flour, mix well, and cook for 5-8 minutes. Add bell pepper, celery, onion, thyme, and bay leaves. Add water, salt, pepper, and Worcestershire sauce, mix well, and let cook on low heat uncovered for the first 45 minutes, then cover and cook for 30 minutes. Then add diced potatoes, cover, cook 20 minutes, and stir every 20 minutes during the whole cook time. Serve with grits or rice. Serves 6-8.

JARDINIERE

¼ lb. lean salt pork or
  bacon, diced
12 small onions, peeled
2 tsp. flour
1 lb. new potatoes, scraped
Small bunch fresh herbs
1 bay leaf

2 tbsp. butter
1 lb. young carrots,
  scraped
2 lb. fresh green peas
  (weigh before shelling),
  shelled
Sugar, salt, and pepper

Brown salt pork or bacon in the butter in a heavy pan. Add carrots and onions and cook for about 3 minutes. Sprinkle flour into the pan and then add enough hot water to cover. Add bay leaf. Put lid on the pan and cook slowly 15 minutes. Next put in the peas, potatoes, herbs, a little sugar, salt, and pepper to taste. Simmer for another 25 minutes. Serves 6.

SHORT RIBS IN WINE

6 large short ribs
1½ cups dry red table wine
1 tsp. salt
1 bay leaf
1 onion, thinly sliced
Minced parsley

Instant meat tenderizer
1 8-oz. can tomato sauce
½ tsp. crumbled sweet
  basil
Cornstarch or flour

Use instant meat tenderizer on short ribs according to label directions. Brown meat well in large Dutch oven. Pour in wine, tomato sauce, salt, basil, onions, and bay leaf. Simmer until meat is tender, about 1½ hours. Remove meat to warm platter and keep hot. Skim fat off juices, then thicken juice with cornstarch or flour paste. Sprinkle meat with minced parsley.

BEEF AND PORK LOAF

1¼ lb. ground beef
2 cups (2 to 3 slices) soft
   bread
¼ cup (about 1 small)
   minced onion
¼ tsp. pepper

½ lb. ground pork
1 cup milk
1 egg, well beaten
2 tsp. salt
1 tsp. monosodium
   glutamate

Mix together all ingredients lightly and pack lightly into 9½ x 5¼ x 2¾ inch loaf pan; shape rounded top. Bake at 350°, 1 to 1½ hours. Completely cool meat loaf in pan on rack. Gently loosen edges of meat loaf with a spatula and invert pan; remove pan. Cool and refrigerate meat loaf. For packed lunch, wrap cold slices in waxed paper, moisture-vaporproof material, or aluminum foil or use in sandwiches.

CHUCK WAGON PEPPER STEAK

1 3-lb. round bone arm chuck
   roast, 2" thick
2 tbsp. instant minced onion
2 tsp. marjoram
1 cup white vinegar
3 tbsp. lemon juice
2 tsp. thyme

2 tsp. unseasoned meat
   tenderizer
1 bay leaf, crushed
½ cup salad oil
¼ cup peppercorns,
   crushed, or 2 tbsp.
   cracked pepper

Pierce steak deeply with fork. Place in shallow baking pan. Combine remaining ingredients except pepper; pour over meat. Let stand at room temperature for 1 to 2 hours (no longer). Remove from marinade. Pound in cracked pepper on each side. Grill until done. Serves 6.

BOILED BEEF

Combine 1 lb. short ribs of beef, 2 onions, 2 carrots, and 1 stalk of celery (all sliced), 3 sprigs of parsley, 5 peppercorns, ½ tsp. salt, and 4 qt. of water. Bring the liquid to a boil, skim off the scum, and simmer the stock for an hour. Bring the stock to a boil, plunge in a 3-pound piece of brisket of beef, and skim the stock again after it returns to a boil. Reduce the heat and simmer the beef, covered, leaving just enough space for steam to escape, for 2 to 2½ hours. Serve the meat very hot, with cold beet salad and potato dumplings. Serve caper, mushroom, tomato, or horseradish sauce separately. Serves 3-4.

BEEF, TOMATO, AND CABBAGE SCALLOP

1 lb. ground beef or
  other lean meat
2 tbsp. shortening
¼ cup chopped onion
1 cup chopped celery
1 clove garlic, minced
Bread crumbs

2½ cups canned or fresh
  chopped tomatoes
Salt and pepper to taste
4 cups chopped or
  coarsely shredded
  cabbage
2 tbsp. butter

Brown meat in shortening. Add onion, celery, and garlic. Cook 5 minutes. Add tomatoes and seasoning. Simmer 5 minutes longer. Place alternate layers of cabbage and meat mixture in a 1½-quart casserole. Top with bread crumbs. Dot with butter. Bake in 375° oven 45 minutes. Serves 6.

BOEUF A LA MODE

Boeuf à la Mode is a pot roast prepared the French way. Its special flavor—the reason why it is so delicious—depends upon the wine marinade in which it soaks before cooking. It penetrates the meat, is then used for the cooking liquid, and finally goes into the sauce. If one is in a hurry these hours of marinating the meat can be omitted, in which case, the wine and spices are added to the pan after the meat has been browned. Do be particular, however, when you remove the meat from the marinade, to wipe it as dry as possible—if it is wet it will not brown well. Be careful, too, about adding the salt because as the liquid cooks down the salt in it becomes more pronounced. If you happen to have your oven going when the time comes to brown the meat, put it in the oven and baste it often with the fat. That gives it a fine even brown.

4-5 lb. rump of beef	5-6 carrots parboiled and
Larding pork	cut in pieces
1 tbsp. salt	12 small onions (or 3
Pepper	large, cut in quarters)
1 pt. wine (white or red)	browned in a little butter
2 tbsp. fat	1 qt. stock or water
2 tbsp. flour	1 cup tomatoes
1 veal bone (or calf's foot)	1 clove garlic
1 faggot	

Lard beef with strips of larding pork. Season it with salt and pepper and put in a bowl with the wine. Let marinate in a cold place 5-6 hours, turning the meat over several times, the better to absorb the wine. At the end of this time, put fat in saucepan and heat very hot. Remove meat from wine and dry it well all over, then brown in hot fat on all sides.

When golden brown, drain fat from pan, sprinkle flour in bottom of pan, and mix it with the brown juice which clings to the pan. Add bone, marinade, stock (or water), tomatoes, garlic, and faggot. The meat should be just covered with liquid, but no more.

Bring to boil, cover pan, and cook slowly on top of stove or in moderate oven of 350° about 2 hours. Remove meat from gravy and skim off all fat. Return meat to pan and put back to a boil. Cook 1½ to 2 hours longer or until meat is tender. Test by piercing with a fork and if it offers no resistance it is tender. Remove veal bone (if used) or if calf's foot is used cut meat in small pieces and serve with the beef. Arrange carrots and onions around dish. Correct the seasoning of the gravy, which should have reduced to about half the original quantity. May be served either hot or cold. If served cold, the veal bone should be included so that the gravy will become jellied. Serves 6-8.

BOEUF A LA MODE EN GELEE

2-4 cups beef stock, fresh
  or canned
3 envelopes unflavored
  gelatin
½ tsp. lemon juice
½ bay leaf

1 tsp. salt
3 egg whites
½ tsp. dried thyme
10 peppercorns
½ cup dry Madeira

To prepare the cold version of Boeuf à la Mode, let the beef cool for an hour in the braising liquid, turning it once or twice. Transfer the beef to a platter, let it cool to room temperature, then wrap and refrigerate. Strain the braising liquid; cook, cover, and refrigerate it. Cool, cover, and refrigerate the baked onions and carrots.

When the braising liquid is thoroughly chilled, carefully remove and discard all of the fat that has solidified on the surface. In a 2- or 3-quart saucepan, melt the braising liquid over low heat and then measure it. Add enough beef stock to make 5 cups in all and return it to the pan.

Soften the gelatin in an additional 1 cup of cold fresh stock, and add it. Beat the egg whites to a froth with a wire whisk and stir them into the stock, together with the lemon juice, thyme, bay leaf, peppercorns, and salt.

Bring to a boil over moderate heat, stirring constantly. When the aspic begins to froth and rise, remove the pan from the heat. Let it rest off the heat for 5 minutes, then strain it into a deep bowl through a fine sieve lined with a dampened kitchen towel. Allow the aspic to drain without disturbing it at any point. When it has drained completely through, add the Madeira, and taste and season the aspic with more salt if needed.

Pour a thin layer of aspic—about ⅛ inch thick—into the bottom of a large serving platter and refrigerate it until the aspic is set. Then carve the cold beef into ¼-inch slices and arrange the meat, onions, and carrots attractively on the platter. Heat about ¾ cup of the aspic in a small pan just until it melts, then set it in a bowl filled with crushed ice or ice cubes immersed in water. Stir the aspic gently with a metal spoon until it thickens, almost to the point of setting. Working quickly, spread a thin glaze of aspic over the sliced beef and vegetables. Chill until the aspic sets. Repeat this process two more times to make three coatings of aspic—melting and chilling for each layer. Refrigerate the platter until the glaze is firm. Meanwhile, melt the remaining aspic and pour it into a large flat roasting pan to make a sheet of film no more than ¼ inch deep; chill it.

When all the aspic is very firm, remove the roasting pan from the refrigerator and score the sheet of aspic into diamonds with the tip of a sharp knife by cutting crossing diagonal lines about 1 to 1½ inches apart. Arrange the diamonds decoratively around the aspic-covered beef. Chop any scraps into fine dice and garnish the platter with it as fancifully as you like. You can even put the chopped aspic into a pastry bag with a plain tip and press the aspic out in scrolls on the beef.

BEEF BRISKET WITH SAUERKRAUT

4 lb. beef brisket
1 tbsp. salt and pepper
1 cup vinegar
1 uncooked potato, grated

Hot water
1 qt. sauerkraut
3 tbsp. brown sugar

Cover brisket with water, season, and simmer 1½ hours. Add sauerkraut, vinegar, and brown sugar. Cook about 1 hour longer or until meat is tender. Add potato and cook 10 minutes longer. Serves 8.

BEEF TIPS BOURGUIGNON

Bourguignon means the dish has red wine sauce. You can have your butcher cut a cube of beef about ⅛ inch thick, from the hind quarter. The beef tip is the end of the fillet and it costs more but is very tender. You would have to cook the hind longer. When using the tip, the cooking time is cut in half. This dish is just a beef stew. The pearl onions are for garnishing and if you use the water from the onions you will get a greater flavor.

4 lb. beef tips
1 medium yellow onion,
    chopped
6 oz. butter
4 oz. all-purpose flour
3 bay leaves
1 tbsp. salt

2 cloves garlic
1 tbsp. whole thyme
1 cup tomato purée
2 cups Cabernet Sauvignon
2 pt. beef stock
10 oz. pearl onions
1 tsp. white pepper

In heavy pot, place butter, beef tip, yellow onion, and garlic. Cook until beef tips start to turn brown. Add flour; mix well. Add bay leaf, thyme, salt, pepper, tomato purée, beef stock, and Cabernet Sauvignon, stirring constantly. Reduce heat and cook for 45 minutes. Add pearl onions. Check the beef tips to see if tender. Let cook 15 minutes more. May be served with flat noodles. Serves 6-8.

BEEF STOCK

2 ribs celery, chopped
2 carrots, chopped
1 medium yellow onion
5 lb. shin bone, split

1 tsp. thyme
2 bay leaves
6 qt. water

Preheat oven to 475°. Put bone in oven, turning about every 15 minutes until brown. Add celery, carrots, onions, thyme, bay leaves, and water. Reduce the heat to 300°. Let cool until the stock has reduced to 2 quarts and strain.

BLANQUETTE OF VEAL

3 lb. veal brisket
1 carrot
1 tbsp. butter
Yolks of 2 eggs
½ gallon water

2 onions
½ can mushrooms
1 tbsp. flour
Juice of 1 lemon
Salt and pepper to taste

Take the brisket of veal and cut into pieces of 2 square inches. Put in a stew pot and cover with the water. Add salt, pepper, onions, and carrot, chopped fine. Let boil until very tender. When it reaches this stage, take the meat out of the saucepan, and keep the water in which it was boiled. Take another saucepan and put the butter in it, and as it melts add the flour. Mix well, continuing to dissolve until it becomes a smooth cream; do not let it brown. Add one pint of water in which the veal was boiled. Stir well, making it very light and not thick. Add mushrooms, and let the whole boil about 15 minutes, so it can be very light. Then put in the veal, which is already cooked. Let it simmer for about 15 minutes longer, and take off the heat. Add the egg yolks, well beaten with two tablespoonfuls of the gravy. Add lemon juice. Serve hot. Serves 6-8.

JELLIED VEAL

3 lb. veal shanks
1 tbsp. plus 1 tsp. salt
1 onion, stuck with 2 cloves
4 parsley sprigs
2 tbsp. Tabasco
8 hard-boiled eggs
1 oz. Worcestershire sauce

3 3-lb. necks of veal
3 garlic cloves, peeled
1 bay leaf
1 tsp. dried basil
½ tsp. freshly ground
   black pepper

Put the veal shanks, necks, salt, garlic, onion, parsley, bay leaf, and basil in an 8-quart kettle with enough water to barely cover. Bring to a boil. Boil for 5 minutes, skimming off the scum. Reduce the heat, cover, and simmer 2 hours or until tender. Remove veal from pot. When cool enough to handle, strip the meat from the bones and cut into small pieces. Return the bones to the pot with the Worcestershire sauce and Tabasco and simmer for 15 minutes. Strain the broth into a clean pot through a double thickness of cheesecloth. Add the cut-up veal to the strained broth and bring to a boil. Taste and add pepper and more salt if needed. Remove from the heat and allow to cool.

Peel and slice the eggs. Rinse a 2-quart metal mold, such as a ring mold, with cold water. Put in a layer of veal and broth, then a layer of sliced egg. Continue layers until all veal and eggs are used, finishing with the veal and enough broth to cover.

Cover mold with foil and chill 8 hours or more. At serving time, unmold on serving plate and cut into fairly thick slices. Serve with Vinaigrette Sauce as a luncheon dish.

VINAIGRETTE SAUCE

1 tsp. salt
8 tbsp. olive oil

¼ tsp. pepper
2-3 tbsp. wine vinegar

Combine sauce ingredients and mix well. Pour over salad just before serving and toss.

VIENNESE VEAL CUTLETS

Trim 2 veal cutlets—each about ½ inch thick and weighing 1½ lb. Remove the bones and cut the meat into 6 serving pieces. Cut the pieces across the grain of the meat, leaving the little "nut" which is divided from the rest of the cutlet by a thin skin, in a single piece.

Pound each piece thin, until it is as large as 6 inches by 8 inches. Dip the cutlets first in ½ cup of flour then in 2 beaten eggs, and then in 1 cup dry sieved bread crumbs. Sauté them over low heat, a few at a time, in 2 skillets with ¾ cup butter in each for not more than 15 minutes, until they are golden brown on both sides. Keep the cooked schnitzel hot in a very slow oven (250°) until all are done. Serve the Wiener schnitzel with lemon slices topped with anchovy fillets. Serves 6.

SAUTEED VEAL WITH BRANDY AND ARTICHOKES

6 2-oz. veal cutlets
(pounded out)
1 oz. flour (seasoned with
salt and pepper)
18 artichoke hearts cut in
half
4 oz. sliced jumbo
mushrooms

1½ oz. butter
1 oz. brandy
3 oz. butter
½ cup heavy cream
¼ oz. fresh thyme

Dust veal with flour. Sauté in 1½ oz. butter. Remove veal from pan. Add sliced mushrooms. Cook 2-3 minutes. Then add artichoke, brandy, and heavy cream. Cook 2-3 minutes more. Add the cooked veal and thyme, and fold in 3 oz. butter until melted. Do not boil. Place two pieces of veal on each plate. Put mushrooms and artichokes on top of veal. May be served with pasta. Serves 6.

SAUTEED VEAL CUTLETS

Trim 2 veal cutlets—each about ½ inch thick and weighing 1½ lb. Remove the bones and cut the meat into 6 serving pieces. Cut the pieces across the grain of the meat, leaving the little "nut" which is divided from the rest of the cutlet by a skin, in a single piece. Pound each piece lightly; the pieces should be thicker than Wiener schnitzel or Scallopini. Sprinkle the 6 cutlets with salt and dredge them lightly in sifted flour. Sauté them in a large skillet in 4 tbsp. butter for 15 minutes until they are brown on both sides. Keep the sautéed cutlets hot in a very slow oven (250°) until all are done.

Make the following sauce. To the juices in the skillet add ½ cup beef or veal stock, 2 tbsp. butter, the juice of ½ lemon, and ½ tsp. meat extract. Bring the sauce to a boil and pour it over the cutlets. Garnish the platter with lemon wedges and parsley. These are best prepared for a small number of people and served at once, without being kept hot in the oven.

VEAL CUTLETS IN WINE WITH OLIVES

1½ lb. veal round steak (cutlet), cut about ¼" thick
¼ cup flour

½ tsp. monosodium glutamate
1 tsp. salt
¼ tsp. pepper

Wipe with clean damp cloth. To increase tenderness, place meat on flat working surface and repeatedly pound with meat hammer. Turn meat and repeat process. Cut into 6 serving-size pieces. Coat with a mixture of remaining ingredients.

Heat in a skillet over low heat, 2-3 tbsp. butter or margarine. Brown meat over medium heat. Add ⅓ cup Marsala wine and ⅓ cup pitted, sliced green olives. Cover skillet and cook over low heat about 1 hour, or until meat is tender when pierced with a fork. Serves 6.

VEAL KIDNEYS FLAMBE

Remove most of the fat and as much membrane as possible from 2 veal kidneys. Brown the kidneys on all sides in 2 tbsp. hot butter, sprinkling them as they cook with salt and pepper. Turn off the heat, remove the kidneys, and cut them into slices ¼ inch thick, reserving the blood and juices. Return the slices to the pan and heat them slowly.

Heat 2 tbsp. Cognac, ignite the spirit, and pour it over the kidneys. Add 2 tbsp. Dijon-style mustard, the juice of half a small lemon, and the reserved blood and juices. Cook the mixture, stirring over low heat for 2 minutes. Add 2 tbsp. heavy cream and a little chopped fresh tarragon or ⅛ tsp. dried tarragon. Serve the kidneys hot over fluffy rice, noodles, or triangles of toast. Serves 2.

VEAL CHOPS PIZZAIOLA

¼ cup olive oil
6 veal rib or loin chops, cut ½" thick
3½ cups (#2½) can tomatoes (sieved)

2 cloves garlic, sliced
1 tsp. salt
½ tsp. chopped parsley
1 tsp. oregano
½ tsp. pepper

Set out large, heavy skillet having a tight-fitting cover. Heat olive oil in skillet. Wipe veal with a clean cloth and then slowly brown on both sides in skillet. Meanwhile, combine remaining ingredients. Slowly add tomato mixture to browned veal. Cover skillet and cook slowly for 45 minutes or until meat is tender when pierced with fork. Serves 6. *To sieve tomatoes*: Force tomatoes through coarse sieve or food mill. *To clean garlic*: Separate into cloves and remove outer (thin, papery) skin.

WIENER SCHNITZEL

8 thin 3-oz. veal cutlets
1 cup flour
1 cup fine bread crumbs
1½ tsp. salt

2 eggs
½ cup butter
⅛ tsp. pepper
Water and milk

Pound the cutlets with a meat hammer or the edge of a heavy saucer until they are tender. Mix the pepper and salt with the bread crumbs, blending them thoroughly. Beat the eggs lightly after adding 1 tbsp. water or milk for each egg. Cut the cutlets into serving-size portions, dredge them in flour, and dip them into the beaten egg mixture and seasoned bread crumbs. Fry them quickly on both sides in hot butter and serve at once. Serves 4.

VEAL SCALLOPINI

8 thin scallops of veal
¾ cup dry bread crumbs
1 tsp. dry mustard
1 tbsp. Worcestershire sauce
½ cup beef broth or dry
   white wine

1 egg, slightly beaten
5 tbsp. butter or margarine
½ tsp. salt
¼ tsp. pepper

Dip scallops in beaten egg; coat with bread crumbs. Let stand 10 minutes to dry (this helps keep coating on during cooking). Brown scallops on both sides in 3 tbsp. butter or margarine in skillet or chafing dish. Remove scallops; keep warm. Add to pan remaining 2 tbsp. butter or margarine, mustard, salt, pepper, Worcestershire, and beef broth or wine. Stir to loosen any brown bits on sides and bottom of pan. Heat to boiling. Serve sauce over hot scallops; sprinkle with parsley. Serves 4.

VEAL STEAKS PARMESAN

2 veal steaks (about 2 lb.)
2 tbsp. butter
1½ cups sliced mushrooms
3 tbsp. sherry
2 tbsp. Parmesan cheese

Pinch garlic powder
1 medium onion sliced
1 tbsp. butter
Salt and pepper
Pinch oregano leaves

Lightly brown veal in 2 tbsp. butter in heavy skillet on both sides. Remove to heated dish. Add sliced onions and mushrooms to skillet. Stir until pan juices are absorbed. Add 1 tbsp. butter and blend well. Cook, covered, until onion is soft.

Add veal, garlic, and sherry. Lightly salt and pepper veal. Sprinkle on Parmesan cheese in equal amounts on each steak. Sprinkle on oregano. Cover and cook over medium heat until veal is fork tender. Remove veal from skillet. Blend onion and mushrooms. Serve in equal amounts over steak. May be served with Bordeaux or Burgundy wine.

VEAL AND PORK EN BROCHETTE

1 lb. veal steak
1 egg
Fat
1¾ tsp. salt
½ cup sour or sweet cream

1 lb. pork shoulder
1 cup fine crisp cereal
  crumbs
½ cup butter
1 cup water

Cut veal and pork into 1½-inch squares. Place 2 squares of pork and 2 of veal alternately on each of several skewers. Dip each into egg, then into crumbs, and brown in butter. Season, add water, cover, and simmer until tender, about 1 hour. Remove to hot platter and pour cream into pan. Heat to boiling and serve with meat. Serves 8.

VEAL PARMIGIANA

1 cup dry bread crumbs
12 thin scallops of veal
2 eggs, slightly beaten
1 clove garlic, mashed
1 can (1 lb.) tomatoes
2 cans (8 oz. each) tomato
  sauce
½ tsp. leaf thyme, crumbled
2 tbsp. butter or margarine
1 pkg. (8 oz.) mozzarella
  cheese

¼ cup grated Parmesan
  cheese
1 cup chopped onion
2 tbsp. pure vegetable oil
1½ tsp. basil, crumbled
½ tsp. salt
½ tsp. onion salt
¼ tsp. pepper
½ cup grated Parmesan
  cheese

Mix bread crumbs and ¼ cup Parmesan cheese in shallow plate. Dip veal pieces in beaten eggs; coat well with crumb mixture. Let stand to dry (this helps keep coating on) while preparing sauce. Sauté onion and garlic in oil in saucepan until soft. Add tomatoes, tomato sauce, basil, thyme, salts, and pepper. Cover; simmer 15 minutes.

Heat oven to 350°. Heat 2 tbsp. oil and butter or margarine in skillet until mixture foams. Add veal scallops, a few at a time, and brown on both sides. Add more oil or butter or margarine if needed. Cut mozzarella cheese into 12 slices. Spoon some sauce into shallow baking dish. Arrange alternate, overlapping slices of cheese and scallops in dish; spoon remaining sauce. Sprinkle with ½ cup Parmesan cheese. Bake 15 to 20 minutes or until sauce bubbles and cheese melts. Serves 6.

SWEETBREAD MONTGOMERY

Slice sweetbread ¼" thick lengthwise. Cook after dipping in egg and bread crumbs. (Bread crumbs must be made without crusts.) Place the sweetbread on a round platter in the form of a crown. Place fresh asparagus tips cooked in butter in the center of the crown.

A supreme sauce (thick white sauce and heavy cream) should be served on the side. Place sliced truffles inside of sauce before serving.

VEAL OR LAMB KIDNEYS CHASSEUR

Plunge 6 veal or 12 lamb kidneys into boiling water, drain them immediately, and remove the thin skins and the tough centers. Cut the kidneys into thin slices. Sauté the slices in ½ cup butter until they are lightly browned. Add 1 tsp. each of chopped parsley and onion or chives, and cook the mixture over high heat for 2 minutes. Sprinkle the mixture with 1 tbsp. flour and blend well. Add ½ cup each of Madeira, dry white wine, and beef stock; bring the sauce to a boil. Simmer the mixture over low heat, stirring occasionally, for 5 minutes.

Sauté ½ lb. mushrooms, thinly sliced, in ¼ cup butter until they are soft. Add them to the kidneys and cook the mixture for 3 minutes. Serve the kidneys garnished with parsley and triangles of toast.

ROAST VENISON

10 lb. venison
2 cloves garlic, chopped
1 medium yellow onion, chopped
½ bell pepper, chopped
5 bay leaves
2 cups water

1 bottle red wine
5 cups white wine
1 tbsp. thyme leaf
1 tbsp. rosemary
2 oz. green pepper sauce
2 tbsp. salt

Combine all the ingredients above together (except venison) for the marinade. Place the venison in the marinade 24-40 minutes.

Preheat oven to 375°. Remove the venison from the marinade and place in roasting pan. Put in oven, then put the marinade in a pot and let come to a boil. Skim off top. Let simmer to half the amount then start basting the roast, about every 15 minutes. Cook the roast 12 minutes per pound. Strain the sauce and serve with the roast. Serves 6-8.

VEAL FRICASSEE JARDINIERE

2 lb. veal rump
Fat
1 tsp. minced parsley
2 carrots, sliced
½ cup sliced celery
1 cup chopped peas or
  mushrooms

2 tbsp. flour
Salt and pepper
2 bay leaves, minced
1 cup water or stock
2 onions, chopped

Cut veal into 1-inch cubes, dredge in flour, and brown in fat. Season and add parsley, bay leaves, carrots, water, celery, and onions. Cover tightly and cook in moderate oven (350°) 45-60 minutes, or until meat is tender. Remove veal. Add peas and thicken liquid with flour mixed with a little cold water. Cook until thickened. Pour over veal. Serves 4 to 6.

VEAL SCALLOPINI WITH MADEIRA WINE, ALMOND RICE, AND PETIT POIS

1½ lb. veal in 2 oz. slices
1 cup flour
4 oz. fresh mushrooms,
  sliced
½ pt. beef stock
4 oz. Madeira wine

1 cup rice
Butter
½ cup petit pois peas
¼ cup toasted slivered
  almonds

Dust veal in flour and brown in butter on both sides. Sauté mushrooms. Combine veal and mushrooms. Add half of beef stock; let simmer with cover on pan at least 5 minutes. Add other beef stock and half of wine. Let simmer for 15 minutes. Before serving add rest of wine. Boil rice in water until medium done. Drain until thoroughly dry. Add butter, peas, and almonds. Fluff and heat thoroughly. Serve hot with veal. Serves 4.

VEAL IN MUSHROOM CREAM SAUCE

Sprinkle 4 veal medallions cut from the loin, each about ½" thick, with salt and white pepper and dredge them in flour, shaking off the excess. In a stainless steel or enameled skillet, heat 3 tbsp. unsalted butter over moderately high heat until the froth subsides. Add the veal, and sauté it for 1 minute and 30 seconds on each side, or until it is springy to the touch.

Transfer the veal with a slotted spoon to a platter and keep it warm. Pour off the fat from the skillet, add to the skillet ¼ cup Madeira and 2 tbsp. brandy, and deglaze the skillet over moderately high heat, scraping up any brown bits clinging to the bottom and sides. Reduce the liquid to about 2 tbsp., add ½ lb. mushrooms, sliced thin, and 1 cup heavy cream, and reduce the liquid, stirring, until it is thickened slightly and smooth. Add any juices that have accumulated on the platter and season the sauce with salt and white pepper. Pour the sauce over veal.

VEAL SCALLOPS WITH APPLES AND CALVADOS

1½ lb. veal scallops,
  pounded thin, 3 oz. each
2 oz. flour
1 red apple, cored and sliced
1 tbsp. tarragon
3 tbsp. oil

2 tbsp. butter
4 tbsp. Calvados
¼ cup heavy cream
Salt and pepper to taste
1 cup chicken stock

Heat the oil and dust the scallops with flour. Shake off excess and brown quickly on both sides. Remove from the pan and discard the oil. Add the butter to the same pan and heat over moderate heat. Add the apple slices and toss for 3-4 minutes. Add the Calvados carefully and flame. Add the stock, cream, and tarragon. Reduce the sauce until thickened and season with salt and pepper. Add the veal and serve. May be served with angel hair pasta. Serves 4.

SAUTEED VEAL WITH THREE HERBS SAUCE

12 pieces veal, 3 oz. each,
  pounded
8 fresh mushrooms, sliced
  (large)
½ tsp. fresh dill, finely
  chopped
½ tsp. fresh rosemary,
  finely chopped
1 tsp. fresh basil, finely
  chopped

1 cup all-purpose flour
1 cup chicken stock
¼ cup heavy cream
4 oz. Madeira wine
½ cup water chestnuts,
  sliced
2 tbsp. butter
Salt and pepper to taste

Dust veal in flour and sauté in butter for 3 minutes per side. Add herbs, sliced mushrooms, and Madeira wine. Cook for 3 minutes, then add water chestnuts, chicken stock, and heavy cream. Cook for an additional 4 minutes. Season with salt and pepper. Serve with angel hair pasta. Serves 4.

PANEED BABY WHITE VEAL

3 3-oz. cuts baby white
  veal, pounded
2 cups heavy cream
1 egg
½ lb. linguine, cooked

1 pt. milk
3 tsp. grated cheese
1 tsp. cracked peppercorns
1½ cups bread crumb mix
¼ lb. butter

Take egg and mix with milk. Put the veal in this wash and pound in the the bread crumbs. Then in sauté pan, put butter and place the breaded veal in it. Brown on both sides about 3 minutes. In another pan, put the heavy cream, and peppercorns, grated cheese, and 2 tbsp. of butter. Stir; do not let boil. Mix the linguine in it. Put the breaded veal on plate with the pasta and serve. Serves 3.

VEAL MEAT LOAF WITH YELLOW MUSTARD

10 oz. ground veal
3 oz. hard French bread
(soaked and drained)
1 tbsp. yellow mustard
1 tbsp. Worcestershire sauce
¼ cup bell pepper, chopped
½ cup yellow onion,
chopped
¼ cup butter

1 tbsp. thyme
1 tbsp. chopped garlic
1 tsp. salt
1 tsp. black pepper
½ bunch green onions,
chopped
1 rib celery, chopped
3 whole eggs

In mixing bowl, mix ground veal and drained French bread well. Add the rest of ingredients except butter; mix well. Grease a flat baking sheet with butter and place meat on it. Mold the meat with the rest of the butter and bake in oven at 450° the first 15 minutes then reduce the oven to 350° for 45 minutes. This meat loaf can be served with tomato sauce or mushroom sauce. Serves 10-12.

SAUTEED VEAL AU CITRON

Veal is a dish we can serve in many ways. The baby white veal doesn't take much cooking. Rather you sauté or pané it (which means, bread it). I have about three veal dishes on the menu but I run a Special at Kabby's for lunch and dinner. I run two Specials daily. Most veal dishes have some kind of wine or brandy. Here's a veal dish that uses wine.

3 3-oz. slices veal (pounded
thin, 3/8")
¼ lb. butter
Lemon
12 large mushrooms, sliced

½ cup flour
¼ cup Madeira wine
Salt
Pepper

Heat sauté pan, dust veal in flour, put butter in pan, then brown on both sides. Take out of pan, put the sliced mushrooms in, and cook for 3 minutes. Add Madeira wine, add 2 oz. unsalted butter and lemon juice, and put the veal in the pan. Add salt and pepper. Cook 3-4 minutes more and serve, garnished with lemon slice. May be served with angel hair pasta. Serves 3.

OSSO BUCO

Osso Buco is veal shank, cut one-half inch thick. This recipe was popular in the coffee shop at the Pontchartrain Hotel. I serve it in Kabby's at the Hilton also. I fix it for Sunday Brunch. Some chefs use white wine, but I use red wine because I think you get a better flavor.

Tip: Use the shank portion—it doesn't take as long to cook. Watch for size, because in the end you get nothing but bone.

6 7-oz. veal shanks, cut ½" thick
½ cup tomato purée
2 ribs celery, cut lengthwise
1 carrot, cut lengthwise
2 cups red wine
¼ cup oil
2 oz. jalapeno pepper sauce
2 cloves garlic, chopped
2 tbsp. flour

1 medium bell pepper, sliced
1 medium yellow onion, sliced
4 bay leaves
1 tsp. salt
½ tsp. black pepper
5 cups chicken stock
2 tbsp. rosemary

Salt and pepper the veal shanks. Set oven at 450°. Put shank in a flat pan and leave in oven for 20 minutes. Add oil and flour; mix well. Let cook for 15 minutes more, then add bell pepper, celery, onion, carrot, garlic, bay leaves, tomato purée, wine, chicken stock, pepper sauce, and rosemary. Reduce heat in oven to 350° and cook 1 hour. Do not cover. Stir every 15 minutes. May be served with pasta.

VEAL GRILLADES A LA CREOLE

24 oz. veal, cut in 8 pieces, pounded out
½ medium yellow onion, chopped
1 medium green bell pepper, chopped
⅓ lb. butter
1 cup all-purpose flour
1 pt. tomato purée

1 tsp. salt
⅓ tsp. white pepper
½ tbsp. thyme
2 bay leaves
⅓ tbsp. brown sugar
1 oz. Worcestershire sauce
2 cloves garlic, finely chopped
1 pt. beef stock

Melt butter in sauté pan. Dust veal in flour and place in pan; brown on both sides. Remove from pan and set aside; in same pan add chopped garlic, onion, and bell pepper. Cook for 5-8 minutes. Add tomato purée, beef stock, bay leaves, sugar, thyme, Worcestershire sauce, white pepper, and salt; mix well and simmer for 20 minutes. Add veal to the sauce; cook for an additional 15 minutes. Serve with grits. Serves 4-6.

BAKED HAM WITH FRUIT SAUCE

12-14 lb. ham
1 lb. brown sugar
6 oz. dry mustard
1 can #303 fruit cocktail

8 oz. sherry wine
2 oz. cornstarch
8 oz. water

Remove skin from ham and trim fat. Score the ham and bake, dry, in 350°-375° oven for 45 minutes to 1 hour.

Mix brown sugar and dry mustard; add water. Brush mixture over ham and return to oven, basting constantly with brown sugar and mustard mixture for 45 minutes. Add wine and fruit cocktail and return to oven for 10 minutes.

Dilute cornstarch with water, add to fruit sauce, and serve. Serves 8.

HINES HICKORY-SMOKED HAM

1 12-14 lb. hickory-smoked
  ham
6 medium onions, sliced
2¾ cups brown sugar
2 cup cider vinegar or
  cooking wine

2 bay leaves
24 whole cloves
1 cup dry bread crumbs
2 tsp. dry mustard
1 tsp. ground cloves

Cover ham with cold water; soak 1-3 days, changing water frequently. Scrub ham; place on rack, skin side down, in a large kettle. Cover with cold water. Add onions, 2 cups brown sugar, vinegar, bay leaves, and whole cloves. Bring to boiling; simmer 20-25 minutes per pound. When small bone at hock end can be twisted out, ham will be done.

Let ham cool in water. Remove skin; cut off some of fat. Score fat. Mix remaining ¾ cup sugar, bread crumbs, mustard, and cloves. Pat on ham while fat is moist. Bake at 400° for 25 minutes or until ham is glazed and brown. Cut ham in very thin slices when serving. Serves 8.

HAM STEAK WITH RED-EYE GRAVY

Brown medium-thick slices of country ham in a skillet without shortening, turning them often. Remove the ham to a plate. Add ½ cup strong black coffee to the pan drippings, stir, and return the ham to the skillet. Cook the ham until the gravy separates into two layers: a reddish brown sauce on bottom and clear ham fat on top. Blend the mixture and pour it over the fried ham.

BARBECUED PORK CHOPS

6 pork chops
12 tbsp. barbecue sauce for
  spareribs

Brown chops on both sides in skillet. Spread 1 tbsp. of sauce on top on each chop. Cover and cook very slowly for 5-8 minutes. Turn chops and put 1 tbsp. of sauce on other side of each chop. Cover and cook very slowly until tender, 30-40 minutes. Turn chops several times so that they are thoroughly covered with sauce. Serves 6.

SPARERIBS WITH SWEET POTATO STUFFING

2 cups mashed sweet
  potatoes
1 cup cooked rice
2 tbsp. melted fat

4 lb. spareribs
1 tbsp. minced onion
1½ cups minced celery
Salt and pepper

Mix all ingredients except meat thoroughly. Break spareribs through the center and remove any surplus fat. Spread potato mixture on bony side of half of ribs, fold in center to cover filling with other half of ribs. Place in baking pan with heavy meat on top. Season meat and dredge with flour. Cover bottom of pan with boiling water and cook in moderate oven (325°) 1½ to 2 hours or until tender. Serves 4.

PORK WITH BARBECUE SAUCE

12 slices roast pork
½ cup chopped onion
½ cup chopped celery
1 clove garlic, minced
⅓ cup chili sauce
¼ cup cider vinegar
2 tbsp. brown sugar
¾ tsp. salt

¾ tsp. chili powder
½ cup water
¼ cup Worcestershire sauce
¾ tsp. monosodium
   glutamate
⅛ tsp. pepper
6 hamburger buns
¼ cup butter or margarine

Heat pork in skillet over low heat. To chop onion, cut off root end and a thin slice from stem end; peel and rinse. Add onion, celery, and garlic to skillet and cook over medium heat, occasionally moving and turning with a spoon. Cook until onion is transparent. Add remaining ingredients (except buns and butter), cover, and simmer until thoroughly heated.

Meanwhile, split the buns into halves and toast. Spread with butter or margarine. Place pork slices on bun halves and spoon some of the sauce over the meat. Serve at once with remaining sauce. Serves 6.

SPARERIBS AND SAUERKRAUT

Set out a large saucepot or kettle having a tight-fitting cover. Wipe with a clean, damp cloth 3 lb. spareribs, cracked through center. Cut into serving-size pieces. Put spareribs into the saucepot with water to barely cover. Add ½ tsp. salt. Add contents of 1 #2½ can (about 3½ cups) sauerkraut. Cover and bring liquid rapidly to boiling. Reduce heat and simmer 1½ to 2 hours or until meat is tender. Drain slightly and remove to a heated platter. Serve spareribs with the sauerkraut, boiled potatoes, and pickled beets. Serves 6.

MARINATED PORK BUTT

5-6 lb. pork butt
½ bottle red wine
2 carrots, cut lengthwise
3 ribs celery, cut lengthwise
1 medium bell pepper, sliced
2 oz. green pepper sauce
2 tsp. salt
4 cups water
1 oz. horseradish mustard

½ bottle vermouth wine
4 bay leaves
1 medium yellow onion, sliced
2 tsp. rosemary
Cayenne pepper
1 tsp. black pepper
1 clove garlic, chopped

Mix all of the above together except pork, salt, and black pepper.

Trim as much of the fat from pork as possible; add a little salt and black pepper. Stick some garlic in. Put the remainder of the salt and black pepper in the marinade. Put the pork in the marinade for 8-12 hours. Take out, set oven at 350°. Put the pork in a dry roasting pan, leave in oven for 30 minutes, then add the vegetables around it and pour in half of the marinade if you want a thick sauce. Add 2 tbsp. all-purpose flour with 2 tbsp. oil. Let cook on low heat for 10 minutes and add marinade to the mix. If it gets too thick add more water. You should cook the roast about 45 minutes to 1 hour more. Baste every 15 minutes. Serves 6-8.

BOILED SWEET PICKLED PORK

3 lb. pickled pork
1 white onion, chopped
¼ bell pepper, chopped
1 rib celery, chopped

1 gallon water
1 tsp. cayenne pepper
2 bay leaves
1 tsp. allspice

Place the pork in the cold water. Add onion, celery, bell pepper, bay leaves, cayenne pepper, and allspice. Cover and cook for 1½ hours on low heat. Serves 6-8.

ROAST PORK LOIN

3 lb. pork loin, bone
   removed
3 carrots, cut in ⅛" pieces
3 ribs celery, cut in ⅛"
   pieces
2 bell peppers, cut in ⅛"
   pieces

2 tbsp. rosemary
1 red apple, quartered
1 tsp. black pepper
3 bay leaves
3 cloves garlic, chopped
2 tbsp. salt

Place bone under the pork loin in roasting pan. Season with salt, pepper, and rosemary. Around loin, place carrots, celery, bell peppers, bay leaves, and garlic. Put in oven at 350°. Cook for an hour and 15 minutes. Serves 6-8.

MEDALLIONS OF PORK IN
APRICOT BRANDY

4 oz. water chestnuts, sliced
2 oz. flour
1 bay leaf
Butter
2 tsp. jalapeno pepper sauce
8 3-oz. medallions of pork
   loin, sliced and pounded
   out

½ bell pepper, sliced
2 cups beef stock
½ medium white onion,
   sliced
1 tsp. salt
Apricot brandy

In saucepan place butter, dust medallions of pork with flour, and cook on both sides. Add sliced onion and bell pepper and cook for 5 to 8 minutes. Add brandy, water chestnuts, salt, beef stock, jalapeno pepper sauce, and bay leaf. Cook for 10 minutes and serve. Serves 4.

PECAN-STUFFED PORK

¼ French bread, soaked
and drained
¼ lb. whole pecans
1 rib celery
1 tsp. thyme leaves
¼ medium bell pepper,
chopped
2 bay leaves
1 tbsp. green pepper sauce

2 pork patties
¼ medium yellow onion,
chopped
¼ tsp. cayenne pepper
1 whole egg
3 oz. ground meat
1 tsp. chopped garlic
1 cup chicken stock

Mash the patties and ground meat well. Place in heavy pan. Cook till browned. Add onion, celery, bell pepper, thyme, and garlic. Cook 3-5 minutes more. Then add the bread and mix well. Add cayenne pepper, chicken stock, bay leaves, green pepper sauce, and pecans. Beat egg; mix in. Set pan aside for the pork.

Cut 4 lb. pork roast (bone removed) in butterfly shape. Pound to ⅛" thick. Spread pecan dressing over it. Then roll tight, and tie with butcher cord. Put bone around roast. Sprinkle roast with rosemary, salt, and pepper. Melt ¼ lb. butter, and pour over roast. Bake at 350° in oven for 30 minutes. Add 1 rib celery, chopped; 1 carrot, chopped; and ½ bell pepper, chopped, around the roast. Let cook for 45 minutes to 1 hour. For gravy, take roast out, add 2 cups water, and reduce heat. Serves 8-10.

CROWN ROAST OF LAMB

Select an entire loin of spring lamb. Have the butcher prepare a 16-rib crown roast by shaping the joint in a semicircle with the ribs outside and then sewing or tying it together to form a crown. Wrap strips of bacon around the lower part of the crown. Fill the center with a savory bread stuffing. Cover the filling with bacon strips feathered or nicked at the sides. Trim the ends of the bones very carefully; they should not be too long. Wrap each bone in a thin strip of bacon or place a piece of raw potato at each bone to prevent it from burning. Place the roast on a rack and sear it for 20 minutes in a very hot oven. Reduce the heat to moderate and roast for 2½ to 3 hours, basting frequently, at first with hot water mixed with equal parts of butter and then with the drippings in the pan. Remove the bacon or potato from the bones when the crown is done, and substitute broiled mushroom caps or paper frills just before serving. Serve very hot with gravy made from the drippings in the pan. Serve with mint sauce and potatoes. Serves 8.

LAMB STEW WITH PARSLEY DUMPLINGS

⅓ cup flour
½ tsp. pepper
3 tbsp. shortening
4 cups hot water
½ tsp. thyme
1 small bay leaf
2 tbsp. flour
1 12-oz. pkg. (2 cups) corn muffin mix
⅓ cup milk

1 tsp. salt
2 lb. boned lamb shoulder cut in 1" cubes
½ tsp. dillseed
2 tbsp. salt
2 tbsp. water
1 10-oz. pkg. frozen mixed vegetables
2 tbsp. chopped parsley
1 egg

Mix together flour, salt, and pepper; coat lamb cubes. Brown in hot shortening in a large heavy kettle. Add the 4 cups hot water. Add seasonings and cover. Simmer gently about 1 hour and 25 minutes. Remove bay leaf. Mix together the 2 tbsp. water and 2 tbsp. flour; stir into stew. Add frozen vegetables; cook 10 minutes.

For dumplings, empty contents of muffin mix package into bowl. Add parsley, egg, and milk. Blend only until dry ingredients are thoroughly moistened. Drop by tablespoons on top of gently boiling stew. Cover tightly; cook 20 minutes longer. Serves 6-8.

IRISH STEW

6 large potatoes, peeled and
cut into 1½" cubes
6 large onions, sliced
3 lb. boneless lamb, cut into
1" cubes

2 tsp. salt
½ tsp. pepper
1 cup water

In heavy saucepan place a layer of potatoes and sprinkle with a little of the salt and pepper. Add a layer of onions and again season. Place a layer of lamb on top and season. Repeat until all of the ingredients are used up; the top layer should consist of potatoes. Pour the water over it and cover. Bring to a boil and cook over low heat for 1½ hours or until the lamb is tender.

Note: This recipe is an authentic one for an Irish stew. In certain localities carrots, celery, and tomatoes are added in additional layers. Serves 6-8.

CHARCOAL-BROILED LEG OF LAMB

Have the butcher bone two 6-lb. legs of lamb and split each leg apart at the heaviest section. The meat should be as uniformly thick as possible. Put the meat in a wide container and cover it with a mixture of 3 cups red wine, 1 cup chopped parsley, and 3 onions, thinly sliced. Marinate the meat for 12 hours, turning it occasionally, and drain and dry it.

Arrange the split legs in 2 basket grills, or hinged broilers, laying them as flat as possible. Brush the legs with olive oil and broil them over hot coals, 3 or 4 inches from the heat, for 10-15 minutes on each side. The lamb should be slightly pink in the center.

Lay the meat on a heated platter and put a few tablespoons of butter on the surface. The butter will blend with the juices when the lamb is sliced. Cut the meat diagonally across the grain in thin slices. Serves 10-12.

SPICY LAMB SHANKS

4 lamb shanks
Flour
1 cup cooked prunes, pitted
½ cup sugar
½ tsp. allspice
3 tbsp. vinegar

Salt and pepper
1 cup water
1 cup cooked dried apricots
½ tsp. cinnamon
¼ tsp. cloves
¼ tsp. salt

Season meat with salt and pepper, dredge in flour, and place in greased baking dish. Cover and bake in moderate oven (350°) until meat is tender, 1¾ to 2 hours. Combine remainder of ingredients, heat to boiling, and simmer about 5 minutes. Drain most of fat from cooked shanks, add fruit mixture to meat, cover dish, and bake in hot oven (400°) for about 30 minutes. Serves 4.

Seafood

In New Orleans, if a restaurant doesn't have seafood it might as well close its doors. I guess the first things you think of are oysters, crabs, shrimp, and crawfish. The Gulf of Mexico supplies us with a lot more — we have speckled trout, flounder, red snapper, and catfish. Most people are used to raised catfish. Of course, drum and sheephead are also available. The redfish has a ban on it, but we still have a lot of fish that we can get fresh everyday.

There are a number of fish that I use in this book and they are all local. Yellowfin tuna is a very good fish, as is grouper (usually I stuff the grouper). Flounder stuffed and baked is one of New Orleans' favorites.

In New Orleans, we do trout many ways but just a plain fillet of trout, sautéed with lemon and butter, would do me just fine. But people like it the other ways so I give the people what they want. One of the seafood dishes I have in this book is Fish Cake à la Buckley, named after my general manager at the Hilton. He was on a diet and couldn't have pepper, so I made this cake and he liked it. Also, salmon, wahoo, mahimahi, and swordfish are available here fresh everyday.

TROUT AND SALMON MOUSSE

½ lb. speckled trout fillets
½ lb. silver salmon
2 pt. half & half cream
½ bunch green onions,
  finely chopped
2 tbsp. arrowroot

5 whole eggs
8 oz. raw chicken livers
1 tsp. Tabasco
1 tsp. yellow mustard
6 egg yolks

Mix all ingredients well in food processor. After mixing, let stand for 2 hours in refrigerator. Take out and pour in 4 oz. soufflé dishes that have been well greased with butter. Fill with mixture to the top and place dishes in a baking pan with cold water (should come near top of soufflé dish). Bake for 45-60 minutes at 375°, remove from oven, and let cool. Serves 8-10.

SAUCE

4 slices beets
2 oz. mayonnaise mixed with
  3 oz. yellow mustard
½ cup fish stock

½ tsp. Dijon mustard
1 tsp. chicken base
½ cup Madeira wine
½ tsp. Tabasco sauce

Mix well in food processor. Place over mousses and serve.

SPECKLED TROUT MARGUERY

2 tbsp. butter, softened
2 tbsp. butter, cut into 1½"
   bits
¼ lb. firm fresh mushrooms
   which have been trimmed,
   wiped with a dampened
   towel, and cut lengthwise,
   including the stems, into
   ¼"-thick slices
¼ cup thinly sliced scallions,
   including 3" of the green
   tops

4 8-oz. speckled trout or
   weakfish fillets, skinned
1½ tsp. salt
1½ cups dry white wine
12 medium-sized uncooked
   shrimp (about ½ lb.)
1 cup Hollandaise Sauce
2 tbsp. coarsely chopped
   black truffles
⅛ tsp. cayenne

Preheat the oven to 350°. With a pastry brush, spread 1 tbsp. of the softened butter on the bottom of a flameproof baking pan large enough to hold the fish fillets in one layer. Cut a piece of wax paper to fit snugly inside the pan and spread one side of the paper with the remaining softened butter. Set wax paper aside.

Scatter the mushrooms and scallions over the bottom of the pan and lay the fish fillets over them, side by side. Sprinkle the tops with 1 tsp. of the salt and pour in the wine. Bring to a simmer on top of the stove, cover the fish with the wax paper, buttered side down, and poach the fish in the middle of the oven for about 20 minutes, or until the fillets are firm to the touch.

Meanwhile, shell the shrimp. Devein them by making a shallow incision down their backs with a small sharp knife and lifting out the black or white intestinal vein with the point of the knife. Wash the shrimp briefly in a colander set under cold running water, spread them on paper towels to drain, and pat them completely dry with fresh paper towels.

In a heavy 6-8" skillet, melt the 2 tbsp. of butter bits over moderate heat. When the foam begins to subside, add the shrimp and stir for 2-3 minutes, or until they are pink and firm to the touch. Set the skillet aside off the heat, and prepare Hollandaise Sauce. When the fillets have cooked the allotted time, use a slotted spatula to transfer them to an ovenproof platter. Strain the poaching liquid through a fine sieve into a small enameled saucepan and boil it over high heat until it has reduced to 2 tbsp. With a wire whisk, beat the liquid into the Hollandaise. Stir in the truffles, the cayenne, and the remaining ½ tsp. of salt, and taste the sauce for seasoning.

Preheat the broiler to its highest setting. To assemble the Speckled Trout Marguery, place three shrimp on each fillet and spoon the sauce over the top, masking the fish completely. Slide the platter under the broiler for 30 seconds, or until the sauce is lightly browned. Serve at once.

STUFFED SPECKLED TROUT

6 7-oz. fillets trout	1 cup sauterne wine
½ lb. shrimp (70-90 count)	1 cup sherry wine
½ lb. butter	4 bay leaves
1 bunch green onions,	Salt
chopped	1 lb. crabmeat
3 cloves garlic, chopped	1 tsp. cayenne pepper
1 pt. heavy cream	1 tbsp. thyme
½ cup flour	½ tsp. rosemary

Lay fillets of trout on chopping board. Take the flat part of your hand and mash the trout as much as you can.

In sauté pan, add butter, garlic, and shrimp and cook for 5 minutes. Add green onions and flour; mix well. Add cream, thyme, rosemary, cayenne, salt, bay leaves, sherry wine, and crabmeat. Reduce heat, cook 15 minutes, take off heat, and let cool. Stuff trout. When you finish, place the trout on flat side, pour sauterne wine in the pan with the trout, and bake at 375° for 25 minutes. Serves 6.

TROUT EUGENE

1 bunch green onions
6-7 oz. tenderloin of
   speckled trout
1 lb. lump crabmeat
1 lb. butter
8 oz. peanut oil
½ bunch chopped parsley

18 shrimp, peeled
2 eggs
1 pt. milk
1 lb. all-purpose flour
4 lemons, sliced
2 oz. Worcestershire

Egg Wash: Mix the 2 eggs with the pint of milk—this is for the fish.

To sauté the trout, place the trout in the egg wash and dust in flour. Heat the oil and ½ lb. butter in a saucepan and add the trout. Brown on both sides and place on a plate.

Chop the green onions in half and place each half in two additional sauté pans. Place the crabmeat in one pan and the shrimp in the other. Put ½ lb. butter, 1 oz. of Worcestershire sauce, and 2 lemons in each pan. Cook for 10 minutes, or until the shrimp are cooked. Put the shrimp and crabmeat mixture over the trout, sprinkle with parsley, and serve. Serves 6. Once you try it, you will want it again. This was named after Eugene Off.

TROUT VERONIQUE

This dish has been served at many of the famous Pontchartrain Hotel's Anniversary Dinners. I used it as an appetizer when I served President Ford and many more. It features trout and white grapes. I have given this recipe to many people and they said it turned out very well. However, some people are worried about the cholesterol because of the Hollandaise Sauce on top.

2 trout fillets (1½-2 lbs.
   each)
1 cup Hollandaise Sauce
Salt and cayenne pepper

1 pt. white wine
Juice of 1 lemon
White seedless grapes

Poach trout in white wine in pan that will cover trout, about 7 minutes, with the lemon juice, salt, and pepper. Remove from poaching liquid and place trout on plate, well drained. Reduce the liquid over high heat to 4 cooking spoons of liquid. Add Hollandaise Sauce and stir briskly. Place grapes (if available) on trout, then the sauce, and glaze quickly in the broiler. Serves 2.

HOLLANDAISE SAUCE

5 egg yolks	1 lb. butter
1½ oz. tarragon vinegar	1 oz. water
Salt and pepper to taste	

Combine egg yolks, water, and vinegar. Beat until frothy and place in a hot water bain-marie. Gradually add melted butter and whip. Add salt and pepper to taste.

TROUT PECAN CHEF LOUIS

4 - 6 oz. speckled trout	¼ cup Southern Comfort
1 egg	1 lemon, squeezed
1 pt. milk	2 tbsp. chopped parsley
½ cup oil	¼ tsp. white pepper
½ cup chopped pecans	1 tsp. salt
½ lb. butter, unsalted	1 cup all-purpose flour
1 oz. Worcestershire sauce	

Mix together egg and milk to make egg wash. Salt and pepper trout. Put the trout in egg wash, then in flour. In sauté pan, put oil and trout and cook 4-5 minutes on both sides or until brown. Take out of pan; set aside. In the same pan, put butter, lemon juice, and pecans (toasted). Add the Worcestershire sauce, chopped parsley, and Southern Comfort, then place over trout. Serves 4. This is one of my inventions. Enjoy!

BOUILLABAISSE

4 large scallops
5 oz. salmon cut into pieces
   lengthwise
4 oysters
6 oz. fish stock
6 oz. dry white wine
1½ oz. sauterne
Fresh basil leaf, cut into
   strips

8 scampi
5 oz. turbot cut into pieces
   lengthwise
Carrots, leek, and celery,
   cut into thin strips
1 pt. heavy cream
1 bay leaf

    Sauté carrots, celery, and leek. Add all the seafood, then add fish stock, white wine, and sauterne. Reduce, then add cream, which has been reduced separately with bay leaf and basil leaf. Serves 4-5.

GRILLED SALMON

2 3-oz. portions salmon,
   sliced
½ oz. jumbo mushrooms,
   sliced
½ oz. Shitake mushrooms,
   sliced

½ oz. Crème Fraîche
   (see index for recipe)
¼ oz. melted butter
¼ oz. white wine
1 oz. butter
1 sprig fresh tarragon

    Brush salmon with melted butter, sear on grill. Finish under broiler for 1 minute. In skillet, combine both mushrooms and wine; simmer until wine is reduced by one-half. Add butter and Crème Fraîche; swirl to incorporate. Place salmon on 12" round plate with starch and vegetable. Top salmon with mushrooms and butter sauce. Garnish with tarragon sprig.

RED SNAPPER DUGLERE

6 6-oz. fillets redfish
3 firm tomatoes, cut in
  quarters
2 bell peppers, sliced
2 cups tomato purée
1 tsp. thyme
3 bay leaves
¼ lb. butter

3 lb. shrimp
3 ribs celery, sliced
1 white onion, sliced
5 cups white wine
¼ tsp. white pepper
1 tsp. sweet basil
1 tsp. salt

In sauté pan add butter, celery, bell pepper, onion, shrimp, bay leaves, thyme, salt, pepper, tomatoes, purée, wine, and sweet basil. Cook for 15 minutes longer on low heat; turn off heat.

2 pt. milk
3 whole eggs, beaten

2 cups all-purpose flour
½ cup oil

In heavy sauté pan, place oil. Place fish fillets in mixture of milk and eggs, then in flour. Place in sauté pan and brown on both sides. Place sauce over the fish and serve. Serves 6. This dish was created in the Caribbean Room for special dinners.

RED SNAPPER CARIBBEAN

This was created when I was the executive chef of the Pontchartrain Hotel. The other "ex chef" had just gotten married and wanted to come over with a party of four for dinner. So I wanted to do something special. I had all these fresh crawfish tails, shrimp, and red snappers so I put this dish together and named it Red Snapper Caribbean because it had all the fruit of the sea. The dish may also be made with redfish.

6 6-oz. red snapper fillets	½ lb. shortening
1 bunch green onions, chopped	1 lb. crawfish tails
	1 lb. butter
6 lemons, cut in quarters	4 bay leaves
2 dozen large mushroom caps	3 oz. salt
1 lb. (21-35 count) shrimp	8 oz. white wine
1 tsp. thyme	1 pt. milk
1 tsp. white pepper	2 lb. flour
3 eggs	1 oz. Worcestershire sauce

Egg Wash: Mix the 3 eggs with the pint of milk. This is for the snapper.

In sauté pan, melt shortening. Place the snapper in the egg wash; dust the snapper in flour. Then place the snapper in sauté pan and cook until brown on both sides. Take out of the pan and place on a plate.

In medium saucepan place butter, shrimp, and mushrooms. Cook for 20 minutes on low heat. Then add green onions, crawfish tails, white wine, juice of lemons, thyme, bay leaves, salt, pepper, and Worcestershire sauce. Cook for 15 minutes more on low heat, stirring constantly. Then pour over red snapper and serve. May be served with Stuffed Tomatoes or parslied boiled tomatoes. Serves 6.

RED SNAPPER WITH CRAWFISH
AND SCALLOPS

I cooked this dish on New Orleans' television show, "Breakfast Edition." Margaret Orr invited me to be on the show. I wanted to do something new, so before I went on, I made this dish for a special in the restaurant. Everyone loved it. Anytime you have fresh crawfish and fresh scallops you always seem to have a winner.

6 6-oz. fillets redfish
½ lb. sea scallops
½ lb. peeled crawfish
1 bay leaf
1 qt. crawfish stock
¼ lb. butter
1 cup white wine
½ tsp. salt
1 pt. milk
2 lb. all-purpose flour

¼ tsp. white pepper
¼ bunch green onions,
  chopped
4 large fresh mushrooms,
  sliced
¼ lb. all-purpose flour
1 cup half & half
1 tsp. thyme
2 eggs
5 oz. shortening

In sauté pan, add butter, chopped green onions, and sliced mushrooms. Cook for 5 minutes. Add scallops, crawfish, and thyme; cook for 5 more minutes. Add ¼ lb. flour; mix well. Add crawfish stock, bay leaf, salt, pepper, half & half, and white wine. Cook for 15 minutes.

In sauté pan, add shortening. Place redfish fillets in mixture of eggs and milk, dust in 2 lb. flour, then place in sauté pan. Brown on both sides over medium heat. Take out of pan and place the crawfish and scallops over the fish and serve. Boiled parslied potatoes may be served with this dish.

RED SNAPPER WITH CRAWFISH SAUCE

6 5-oz. red snapper fillets
½ lb. butter
¼ cup flour
12 large mushrooms, sliced
½ bunch green onions
1 lb. crawfish tails

1 cup Vermouth wine
1½ cups heavy cream
1 tbsp. salt
1½ oz. green pepper sauce
3 bay leaves
1 tbsp. thyme

Bake snapper fillets on sheet pan in oven at 350° for 5-8 minutes. To make sauce, make a light roux in a saucepan with butter and flour. Add mushrooms, green onions, crawfish tails, Vermouth, and heavy cream. Mix well. Add salt, green pepper sauce, bay leaves, and thyme. Cook for 8 minutes. Serve over snapper. Serves 6.

BAKED RED SNAPPER BARATARIA

4 red snappers (7 oz. each)
Salt and pepper
1 bunch green onions, chopped
1 lb. lump crabmeat
½ cup white wine
½ cup cornmeal
1 egg

¼ lb. crawfish
¼ tsp. paprika
1 clove garlic, chopped
½ lb. butter
1 tsp. Worcestershire sauce
Cayenne
1 pt. milk

Bake red snapper with salt, pepper, and paprika on buttered baking pan at 350° for 8 minutes. Set aside.

In a sauté pan, add chopped garlic, butter, crabmeat, green onions, white wine, Worcestershire sauce, and a dash of cayenne pepper. Cook for 8 minutes and place over the snapper.

Take the crawfish tails and put them in an egg-milk mixture. Put in cornmeal that is seasoned with cayenne pepper and salt. Fry the crawfish tails until crisp and place on top of the crabmeat.

RED SNAPPER WITH
CHAMPAGNE AND MUSTARD
SAUCE

2 tbsp. dry mustard
1 bottle champagne
1½ pt. heavy cream
5 fillets red snapper
4 chicken bouillon cubes

3 oz. flour
4 oz. butter
2 oz. green pepper sauce
1 oz. honey
Salt and pepper

Heat a saucepan with butter; add dry mustard. Let cook for 2-3 minutes. Add flour and stir constantly. Pour in the champagne. Add heavy cream, honey, green pepper sauce, and bouillon cubes. Keep stirring—do not boil. Reduce the heat to a simmer. On a sheet pan, salt and pepper the snapper and bake in oven at 375° for 10-15 minutes. Take out and spread the sauce over each fillet. Serves 5.

RED SNAPPER WITH GRAPES

4 6-oz. red snapper fillets
¾ cup cream
½ cup fish stock or
   bottled clam juice
1 tbsp. dillweed
1 tsp. salt
1 tsp. pepper

Flour
3 eggs, beaten
¼ cup oil
½ cup white wine
½ cup white grapes,
   seedless

Dredge the fish in flour and shake off excess. Beat the eggs with ¼ cup cream and pass the fish through. Heat the oil in the pan and cook the fish directly from the egg wash for 4 minutes per side or until brown. Timing will depend on the thickness of the fish. Remove the fish and drain on paper towels and keep warm. Discard the fat from the pan and add the fish stock, white wine, and remaining cream. Boil vigorously for 3 minutes and reduce heat. Cook until the sauce is thickened. Add the dill, grapes, salt, and pepper. Serve over the fish. Serves 4.

RED SNAPPER CHEVILLOT

¼ stalk celery, finely
  chopped
½ white onion, finely
  chopped
3 lemons
¼ cup shortening
White pepper
White anisette
½ lb. all-purpose flour
2 cans hearts of artichoke
  (8-10 count)

1 bell pepper, finely
  chopped
½ bunch green onions,
  chopped
¾ lb. butter
Dash Worcestershire sauce
Salt
6 6-oz. fillets red snapper
4 eggs
2 pt. milk

Sauté celery, bell pepper, green onions, and white onion in sauté pan with ½ lb. butter. Cook for 15 minutes on medium heat. Add salt and pepper. Squeeze 1½ lemons and add with Worcestershire sauce to mixture. Take off heat; add artichoke hearts and white anisette. In another sauté pan add shortening and ¼ lb. butter. Dip red snapper in an egg-milk mixture and dust in flour, then add it to the sauté pan. Cook over medium heat until brown on both sides. Take out of sauté pan and place on serving platter. Cover the fish with the sauce and artichokes. Serve with potatoes or stuffed tomatoes. Garnish with remaining lemons (sliced). Serves 6.

GROUPER CORDON BLEU

New Orleans is known for its fish from the Gulf. Since there's a ban on redfish and a shortage on trout, the restaurants have to bring in other fish, like grouper, swordfish, mahimahi, and wahoo. These are the most popular. Plenty of restaurants use drum, sheephead, flounder, and red snapper. The price is up to $7.50-$8 per pound.

I use most of the above fish at Kabby's. I prepare a grilled fish of the day. I find that the grouper is a good fish to work with. The white grouper is good also. This recipe is particularly delicious.

4 6-oz. fillets grouper
1 lb. crawfish tails
4 egg whites
½ lb. margarine
1 tsp. thyme
1 tsp. basil
1 bunch green onions, finely
  chopped
4 oz. provolone cheese

4 fresh spinach leaves
2 cups mixed bread crumbs
1 tbsp. jalapeno pepper
  sauce
½ clove garlic, finely
  chopped
2 bay leaves
1 tsp. cayenne pepper

Pound grouper fillets with palm of hand. With a knife, lightly slice down the center, making a pocket. Set aside.

In a sauté pan, add margarine and garlic. Cook for 2-3 minutes. Add crawfish, green onions, pepper sauce, bay leaves, basil, thyme, and cayenne. Mix well. Let cool.

Take grouper fillets. Open. Place a 1 oz. slice of provolone cheese in each pocket. Add 1 leaf of spinach and ½ cup crawfish. Dip the whole fillets in egg whites, and roll in mixed bread crumbs. Heat slowly in sauté pan until brown on both sides. Serve and enjoy. Serves 4.

TUNA ROCKEFELLER

Tuna is a fast seller—people seem to eat a lot of it. I find that yellowfin tuna is the best you can buy. You can find this recipe at Kabby's, in the New Orleans Hilton.

7 oz. yellowfin tuna fillet
3 fresh oysters
1½ oz. rockefeller sauce
(see index for recipe)

1 oz. Hollandaise Sauce
1 oz. herbsaint

Poach the oysters in the herbsaint. Place the rockefeller sauce on top of the tuna. Bake at 350° for 5-6 minutes. Then place oysters on top of tuna and ladle Hollandaise over the oysters. Put back in oven 2-3 minutes to glaze. Serve and enjoy. Serves 1.

FISH CAKE A LA BUCKLEY

2 lb. grouper, diced
1 tsp. garlic, finely chopped
Plain bread crumbs
½ tsp. basil leaves
1 whole egg
1 tsp. chicken base

¼ yellow onion, chopped
¼ bell pepper, chopped
1 tsp. thyme leaves
¼ lb. margarine
1 cup fish stock

In sauté pan, put margarine, garlic, bell pepper, and onion together and cook for 5 minutes. Add diced fish, thyme, and basil and cook for 5 more minutes. Add fish stock; mix well. Add chicken base and 1 cup bread crumbs. Mix well and add egg. Mix well again; take off heat to cool. Mold the fish cake with No. 12 ice cream scoop, dust in bread crumbs, and sauté in heavy pan until brown on both sides and serve with tomato sauce. Serves 6-8.

TOMATO SAUCE

48 oz. tomato juice

6 oz. fish bone

Reduce until one-half the amount. Do not put any salt or pepper in it.

POMPANO EN PAPILLOTE

3 medium-sized whole
  pompano
1 cup chopped shallots
2½ cups white wine
5 cups fish stock
1 cup crabmeat
Salt and pepper

2 tbsp. flour
6 tbsp. butter
6 egg yolks
1 cup shrimp (21-25 count)
1 bay leaf
Pinch thyme

Tenderloin pompano and cut into 6 fillets. Cook the head and back in 3 cups stock until tender. Sauté fillets in 2 tbsp. butter and add 2 cups wine; cover and simmer slowly until fillets are tender, about 5-10 minutes.

Sauté crabmeat and shrimp in 2 tbsp. butter. Cook 10 minutes. Add thyme, bay leaf, and 1½ cups fish stock and simmer 10 minutes. In another pan melt 2 tbsp. butter, blend in flour, and stir in remaining fish stock. Add crabmeat, shrimp, and shallots mixture, ¼ cup white wine, stock from fillets, and simmer until thickened. Beat egg yolks and mix in the sauce and remaining ¼ cup wine. Add salt and pepper to taste. Set aside until firm.

Cut 6 parchment paper hearts, 12 inches long and 8 inches wide. Butter paper well. Place sauce on paper, then place 1 piece of fillet in each half of bag and fold over half. Seal edges of paper by folding over and pinching together all around. Lay sealed hearts on a buttered baking sheet and bake at 450° for about 15 minutes, or until paper hearts are brown. Serve at once. Cut paper open at table. Serves 6.

BLACKENED CATFISH

4 9-12 oz. catfish fillets
1 oz. thyme
1 oz. garlic, finely chopped
2 oz. cayenne pepper
3 bay leaves
1 oz. oregano

1 oz. black pepper
1 oz. salt
½ lb. butter, melted
1 oz. white pepper
1 oz. onion salt

Combine all the above ingredients together, except catfish, in blender until smooth. Dredge catfish through mixture; shake excess. Heat a heavy fry pan, sprinkle the fish with melted butter, and fry until black on both sides. Remove fish from pan and finish in a preheated oven at 350° for 8-10 minutes. Serves 4.

MARINATED CATFISH LOUIS

6 catfish fillets, 7-9 oz.
1 tsp. oregano
2 tsp. garlic, finely chopped
2 cups olive oil
2 oz. green pepper sauce
2 tsp. paprika

1 tsp. basil
4 bay leaves
1 tsp. thyme
2 tsp. dry mustard
2 tsp. salt
½ tsp. cayenne pepper

Mix all marinade ingredients above together, then place catfish in the marinade. Allow to set for 2 hours and bake in oven at 350° for 10-12 minutes. Set aside. Place sauce on plate and fish on top of sauce. Serves 6.

SAUCE

½ lb. crawfish tails
½ tsp. thyme leaves
½ tsp. oregano leaves
½ cup Vermouth
2 oz. green pepper sauce
3 bay leaves
½ tsp. basil leaves
½ cup dry sherry wine
2 pt. chicken stock
1 medium butternut squash,
  diced ⅛"

1 oz. flour
½ tsp. cayenne pepper
1 oz. Worcestershire sauce
1 medium eggplant, peeled
  and diced ⅛"
1 oz. butter
1 cup heavy cream
½ bunch green onions,
  chopped
1 tsp. salt

Place chicken stock in pot, bring to a boil, and reduce heat. In another pot, place butter and allow to melt. Add flour and mix well; do not brown. Add butternut squash and cook for 5 minutes. Add diced eggplant, chicken stock, green pepper sauce, bay leaves, thyme, basil, cayenne pepper, oregano, Worcestershire sauce, green onions, sherry, Vermouth, and mix well. Cook on low heat for 8 to 10 minutes. Add crawfish tails, heavy cream, and salt. This sauce can be used over the fish or served with pasta.

Note: The butternut squash is to be marinated in pineapple juice, apple juice, honey and cinnamon before adding to sauce.

For garnish, use parslied potatoes, mushrooms, and fresh whole green beans with gold and red bell pepper.

BARBECUED CATFISH

4 9-12 oz. catfish fillets
4 oz. Italian dressing
1 oz. thyme (whole)
3 green onions, chopped

2 oz. lemon juice
3 oz. Cajun powder
1 oz. basil (whole)

Sear catfish fillets on grill. Mix all other ingredients together. Marinate the fish in the mixture overnight. Take out of mixture and bake in oven at 350° for 15 minutes. Serves 4.

BRONZED CATFISH

4 9-12 oz. catfish fillets
1 oz. thyme
1 oz. garlic, finely chopped
½ oz. paprika
1 oz. white pepper
1 oz. onion salt

1 oz. black pepper
1 oz. salt
½ lb. butter
1 oz. cayenne pepper
3 bay leaves
1 oz. oregano

Combine all the above ingredients, except catfish, in blender until smooth. Dredge catfish through mixture on one side. Heat a sauté pan with enough butter to cover the pan. Sauté the fish on the side dredged with mixture for 3 minutes. Remove from pan and finish in preheated oven at 375° for 15 minutes. Serves 4.

AMBERJACK LA PLACE

Amberjack is a good firm fish. The first time I saw one, I was invited over to Florida to cook New Orleans-style food and the fish they gave me to cook was amberjack. They had crawfish and tasso ham, so I combined the two. Now I use amberjack at Kabby's. I had it on the menu but it became difficult to find so I had to take it off. When I'm able to purchase it, I grill or bake it. Very delectable.

4 6-oz. amberjack fillets	**¾ oz. tasso ham, diced**
1½ cups crawfish tails	**¾ cup mustard**
1 cup heavy cream	**½ lb. margarine**

Bake amberjack fillets on flat pan with margarine on top for 10 minutes at 350°. Set aside. In a sauté pan, put tasso ham, heavy cream, mustard, and crawfish tails together and cook for 10 minutes on low heat. Then spread the sauce over the fish fillets and serve. Serves 4.

STUFFED WHOLE FLOUNDER WITH SHRIMP AND CRABMEAT

In New Orleans, flounder was plentiful until lately. It looks like it may be on the rise again. Restaurants serve them whole or stuffed. Most people like them but are afraid of the bones. Some of the restaurants bone them, some don't, and others take out the center bone. If you tenderloin it, you don't have much left. Most chefs don't have time to bone them. This recipe is served at Kabby's. Enjoy.

3 whole flounder
½ bell pepper, chopped
½ lb. butter
1 rib celery, chopped
1 lb. crabmeat
½ bunch green onions,
  chopped
1 tbsp. thyme

½ cup Parmesan cheese,
  grated
2 cloves garlic, chopped
½ lb. shrimp (70-90 count)
½ loaf stale French bread,
  soaked and drained
¼ tsp. cayenne pepper

Debone flounder and place on baking dish. For stuffing, in sauté pan put butter, garlic, celery, green onions, bell pepper, and shrimp. Cook for 10 minutes. Add soaked French bread, thyme, cayenne, crabmeat, and mix well. Cook on low heat for 15 minutes. Stuff the flounder. Sprinkle grated cheese over fish. Bake the flounder in oven at 350° for 20 minutes. Serves 6.

CRAWFISH MONICA

1 lb. pasta
1 stick butter
¾ cup chopped green onions

1 lb. crawfish tails, peeled
1 tbsp. Cajun seasoning
1 pt. half & half

Fresh linguine, fettucine, spinach fettucine, egg noodles, or spaghetti is preferred. Cook pasta according to package directions. Drain and chill by running under cold water. Drain thoroughly. Melt butter in a large saucepan and sauté green onions for 2-3 minutes. Add Cajun seasoning and crawfish tails. Sauté 1 minute. Add half & half and cook for 5-10 minutes over medium heat until sauce thickens. Add pasta to pan and toss well. Serve immediately. Serves 4.

CRAWFISH ETOUFFEE

Crawfish Etouffée is another dish that you find in most Creole restaurants. Today, chefs are getting Creole dishes mixed up with Cajun dishes. Everyone thinks the food is supposed to be hot (spicy). I think food should be well seasoned, not spicy to the point where you have to drink water or tears are brought to your eyes. But Crawfish Etouffée is supposed to be a bit spicy. Once you try this recipe you will like it. It is also served in Kabby's.

8 lb. crawfish
6 onions, chopped
⅓ cup chopped celery
½ tsp. tomato paste
½ cup (1 stick) butter
½ tsp. cornstarch

½ cup water
Salt, pepper, and cayenne
2 tbsp. chopped green
 onion tops
2 tbsp. minced parsley

In large container, place enough water to cover crawfish 3-4 inches. Bring to boil; drop in crawfish and remove from heat. Let stand in hot water 5 minutes. Drain, peel, and clean. In large saucepan, sauté onions, celery, and tomato paste in butter until tender. Add crawfish tails. Dissolve cornstarch in water and add to onion mixture, stirring constantly. Season to taste. Bring to boil over medium heat and cook 15 minutes. Add onion tops and parsley. Mix well. Serve with rice. Serves 4.

CRAWFISH EVANS

I am one who always looks for new dishes to prepare. I needed something new for the menu and I had no crawfish dish at the time which was hot. I sampled a dish called Crawfish Cardel and I liked it even though it had catsup in it. So I said to myself, I can do better than that. So, one day I fixed it for Mr. Albert, the owner of the Pontchartrain Hotel. There are three things he doesn't like: onion, cayenne pepper, and sage. This dish has some of this but surprisingly, he liked it. He was having a party later that evening and asked if I could serve it and, of course, I said yes.

1 lb. crawfish tails
1 qt. chicken stock
4 oz. flour
¼ tsp. thyme leaves
¼ tsp. oregano leaves
½ tsp. Worcestershire sauce
¼ cup Vermouth
½ bunch green onions, chopped

2 egg yolks
1 oz. green pepper sauce
3 bay leaves
4 oz. butter
¼ tsp. basil leaves
¼ tsp. cayenne pepper
1 cup heavy cream
¼ cup dry sherry wine
½ tsp. chicken base

Boil crawfish in chicken stock with chicken base for 30 minutes and strain. In another pot melt butter, then add flour and mix well. Add the herbs, Worcestershire sauce, Vermouth, sherry, green pepper sauce, green onions, and cayenne. Cook for 15-20 minutes, then beat egg yolks with cream and add to the mix. Make sure you keep stirring when you put the egg yolks in. Then turn off heat and serve in 6 individual dishes. May be served over pasta. Serves 6.

CRAWFISH AND PASTA

This recipe was created for the annual St. Michael's Special School charity event. I've been involved with this charity for years. We serve approximately 2,500 people each year for the cooking event, which is held for two days during the months of January and February. I also use this dish at Kabby's. It has several possibilities. Instead of using pasta, you can serve the sauce over fish or as a casserole.

1 lb. crawfish
½ bunch green onions, chopped
¼ lb. butter
½ tsp. basil
½ tsp. cayenne pepper
1 cup white Vermouth
4 large mushrooms, sliced

2 tbsp. grated Parmesan cheese
1 clove garlic, chopped
1 qt. crawfish stock
½ tsp. oregano
1 tsp. salt
1 pt. half & half cream
2 tbsp. flour

Sauté green onions, garlic, and mushrooms in butter for 5 minutes. Add flour; cook for 3 minutes more. Add crawfish and crawfish stock; mix well. Add oregano, basil, salt, pepper, Vermouth, and cook for 10 minutes on low heat. Add grated cheese and half & half cream. Cook for another 3 minutes and pour over pasta, prepared as follows.

Place 2 lb. flat pasta in 1 quart boiling water with ½ tsp. salt. Boil for 5 minutes and drain. Rinse with hot water and place on serving plate. Top with sauce. Serves 8-10.

CREOLE SHRIMP AND GROUPER EN BROCHETTE

I created this dish for a luncheon special. I would buy a whole fillet of fish (5-6 oz. for lunch and 7 oz. for dinner) for other recipes. I would have pieces left over, so I cubed them and put them on a spear like a brochette. I added shrimp and made a Creole mix of herbs. Sprinkle this mix over the brochette, grill, and serve with Mushroom Rice.

8 shrimp
8 cubes fish, 1 oz. each
¼ tsp. cayenne pepper
¼ tsp. basil
¼ tsp. oregano
¼ tsp. onion salt

¼ tsp. paprika
¼ tsp. garlic powder
¼ cup cucumber, chopped
¼ tsp. green pepper sauce
1 large clove garlic, sliced

Spear shrimp on brochette, then garlic, then shrimp, then fish until the spear is filled. Mix dry spices and green pepper sauce and sprinkle over the brochette. Grill until brown on both sides. Then place on top of mushroom rice and garnish with chopped cucumber. Serve with stir-fried vegetables. Serves 2.

MUSHROOM RICE

½ cup long grain rice
6 mushrooms, sliced
¼ red pepper, chopped

Chicken stock
Pepper
Butter

Sauté mushrooms in butter. Add rice, red pepper, pepper, and onions. Mix well. Add chicken stock and cover. Stir every 5 minutes. Cook 6-8 minutes.

BARBECUED SHRIMP

1½ qt. olive oil
2 qt. oil
1 oz. rosemary leaves
3 garlic bulbs, cut in half
3 10-oz. beers

1 oz. thyme leaves
1 oz. salt
½ lb. ground black pepper
3 dozen shrimp, heads on
Juice of 1 lemon

In large pot mix olive oil, oil, rosemary, thyme, salt, pepper, garlic, and lemon juice. Bring to a full boil. Remove from heat and let cool. Incorporate beer into mixture. Add shrimp to mixture and let marinate overnight. Cook shrimp in marinade until shrimp turn pink. Serves 4-5.

SHRIMP EN COQUILLE

2 lb. cooked shrimp
2 tbsp. flour
1 cup cream
⅛ tsp. pepper
½ cup catsup
Buttered bread crumbs

1 clove garlic
2 tbsp. butter, melted
½ tsp. salt
Paprika
1½ tbsp. Worcestershire
  sauce

Rub pan well with garlic. Add flour to melted butter, pour the cream on gradually, and cook, stirring constantly until smooth and thick. Add seasonings and shrimp. Fill shells or ramekins. Sprinkle with crumbs; place in a hot oven (400°) to brown for 10-12 minutes. Serves 6.

SHRIMP SAKI

30 jumbo shrimp
3 lemons
½ lb. butter, melted

1 tbsp. paprika
Salt and pepper

Split the shrimp from the back and wash thoroughly under running water. After shrimp are washed thoroughly, place them in a pan completely opened. Season with salt and pepper and sprinkle paprika on each shrimp. Pour the melted butter on each shrimp, then put them in a hot oven for about 8 minutes. Remove from oven and put under broiler for 5 minutes. Strain juice from three lemons in the melted butter and serve with each portion of shrimp. Serves 4.

SHRIMP AND PERNOD WITH PASTA

More and more Pernod is used in shrimp dishes. The flavor is different. The whole idea is to let the Pernod burn out. Once you put the Pernod in the shrimp dish, light it and let some of it burn out. The sweet basil and the oregano combined with the Pernod gives a great flavor. You can use almost any kind of pasta. The larger the pasta, the heavier the meal becomes.

1 lb. peeled raw shrimp
  (21-25 count)
4 large mushrooms
½ qt. shrimp stock
1 clove garlic, finely
  chopped
½ bunch green onions,
  finely chopped
3 bay leaves
1 tsp. chicken base
1 tbsp. green pepper sauce

½ lb. fresh cooked pasta
2 oz. grated Parmesan
  cheese
1 cup Pernod
¼ lb. butter
½ tbsp. oregano (fresh),
  chopped finely
½ pt. half & half
1 oz. all-purpose flour
1 tsp. basil

In sauté pan, combine chopped green onions, garlic, sliced mushrooms, and butter. Cook for about 3 minutes. Add shrimp. Cook for about 5 minutes. Add flour and cook for another 3 minutes. Pour Pernod over this mixture (it will flame), then add shrimp stock, bay leaves, oregano, basil, and green pepper sauce. Add Parmesan cheese, half & half, chicken base, and keep stirring. Cook for another 5-10 minutes, and serve over pasta. Serves 4.

FRIED SHRIMP

4 dozen shrimp, peeled   ½ lb. all-purpose flour
1 lb. cornmeal   1 qt. milk
1 tbsp. salt   8 eggs
1 tbsp. white pepper

Mix milk and eggs. Dip shrimp in this egg wash, then dredge in mixture of remaining ingredients. Fry shrimp. Serves 5.

SHRIMP "21"

Shrimp in New Orleans is special. We have the white shrimp and the brown shrimp. We boil, fry, stuff, and sauté them. There are a hundred different ways to prepare them and we never seem to get enough. This recipe was created for a lady at a luncheon. At her request, I prepared it in the dining room in a flaky pastry shell, with buttered green asparagus. The next year the St. Michael's Special School charity event began. This was the first dish I cooked for them. We served about nine hundred each day. You must try this one.

3 lb. shrimp   1 qt. shrimp stock
½ bunch green onions   6 large mushrooms
2 oz. white wine   2 oz. sherry wine
4 oz. all-purpose flour   ¼ lb. butter
4 oz. half & half   Salt and pepper to taste

Boil shrimp in shrimp stock. Sauté green onions and mushrooms in butter for approximately 5-8 minutes. Add flour and cook an additional 5 minutes, stirring constantly. Add shrimp, stock, sherry, and white wine. Heat cream and add to shrimp mixture slowly. Add salt and pepper to taste. Cook for 15 minutes. Serves 10.

SHRIMP AND SCALLOP SALAD

¾ lb. shrimp (21-25 count)
  peeled and deveined
2 tsp. Dijon mustard
½ cup safflower oil
½ tsp. salt
2 tbsp. chopped dill
¾ lb. sea scallops

3 tbsp. white wine vinegar
3 tbsp. olive oil
¼ tsp. ground pepper
3 heads bibb lettuce
¼ tbsp. basil
⅓ cup lemon juice

Put a pot of water to a boil. Add the shrimp and scallops. When the water returns to a boil, drain the seafood into a colander. Rinse under cold running water until cool. Slice the shrimp in half, cut the scallops horizontally into 2 or 3 rounds. In a large bowl, blend together the lemon juice and mustard. Gradually whisk in the safflower and olive oils and vinegar. Season with the salt, pepper, and herbs. To serve, arrange the lettuce leaves on a serving plate. Whisk the vinaigrette into the seafood and toss to coat. Arrange the dressed seafood on top of the lettuce. Very popular salad. Serves 4.

BAY SHRIMP IN SOUR CREAM
WITH MUSHROOMS

8 oz. bay shrimp
4 tsp. horseradish
Cognac to taste
Lettuce leaf

12 tbsp. sour cream
Julienned mushrooms
Chopped parsley

In a stainless steel mixing bowl, combine bay shrimp and sour cream. Then add horseradish. Dash with Cognac and add julienne of mushrooms. Serve in fluted white ramekin dish lined with lettuce leaf. Sprinkle with finely chopped parsley. Serves 1.

SHRIMP CLEMENCEAU

28 peeled shrimp with tails
1 medium potato, diced
1 cup green peas
12 medium mushrooms,
  sliced
2 tsp. olive oil

1 tsp. salt
2 tsp. chopped garlic
1½ cups sherry wine
4 bay leaves
2 tsp. chopped parsley
2 tsp. cayenne pepper

Blanch the diced potatoes, then brown them in hot grease. Set aside. In another pot heat the olive oil and garlic (let garlic cook until it starts to turn brown). Add shrimp, bay leaves, cayenne pepper, salt, and sliced mushrooms. Cook 10-12 minutes. Then add green peas, diced potatoes, chopped parsley, and sherry wine. Mix well and cook for 5-8 minutes more. Serves 4.

SHRIMP MARINIERE

1½ lb. raw shrimp
2 green onions, minced or
  ¼ cup minced onion
2 tbsp. butter
Juice of ¼ lemon
½ cup light cream

2 cups white wine
1 cup oyster water, fish
  stock, or chicken stock
2 tbsp. flour
2 egg yolks
1 tbsp. chopped parsley

Peel and devein shrimp. Combine wine, onions, and oyster water. Bring to a boil, and add shrimp. Simmer about 15 minutes. Melt butter and blend in flour. Gradually add ¾ cup of the wine-oyster water in which the shrimp were cooked, stirring constantly until thickened. Add shrimp and cook 10 minutes, then add lemon juice. Beat egg yolks and mix with cream. Combine with hot shrimp mixture, stirring constantly. Serve on toast points or in ramekins garnished with parsley. Serves 6.

LOBSTER THERMIDOR

2½-lb. lobster
4 tbsp. olive oil
1 medium onion
1 cup sliced fresh
  mushrooms
2 tbsp. butter
2 tbsp. flour
¼ tsp. salt
Pinch cayenne pepper

Additional butter
¾ cup milk
¼ cup cream
2 tbsp. dry mustard
Pinch paprika
2 tbsp. grated Parmesan
  cheese
⅔ cup sherry
Bread crumbs

Split lobster, removing the sac at the back of the head. Put olive oil in a large pan, heat it, and then put the lobster in, split side down. Cover and cook slowly for about 10-12 minutes. Remove the lobster from the pan, remove the meat from the body and claws, and reserve the shell, which should be kept warm.

To the oil the lobster was sautéed in (adding a little more if necessary), add peeled and chopped onion and sliced mushrooms. Let cook until tender.

In another pan, melt 2 tbsp. butter over medium heat. Stir in flour, salt, and cayenne pepper, and when smooth add milk. Stir over the heat until the mixture comes to a boil. Then add this mixture to the mushroom and onion mixture, together with cream, dry mustard, paprika, and Parmesan cheese. Reduce this whole mixture to a thick creamy consistency with sherry. Stir the cut-up lobster meat into the sauce and stuff the lobster shell with the mixture. Sprinkle the top of the lobster with bread crumbs, dot with butter, and put under the broiler to brown. Serve.

SOFT-SHELL CRAB WITH SEA SCALLOPS AND CRAWFISH

This dish was created for "Breakfast Edition" on Channel 6 in New Orleans at the request of Margaret Orr. Soft-shell crabs were in season and she asked me to prepare something with crabs. So I did. Soft-shell crabs are good just about any way you fix them: fried, sautéed, or grilled.

Today most people don't like to use an egg wash. In this recipe, you can just dust the crabs in flour (make sure the flour is all-purpose). If you choose to use the egg wash, the crabs will be crispier, and will brown faster.

2 large soft-shell crabs, cleaned
1 cup sea scallops
1 tsp. salt
1 whole lemon, cut in half
1 tbsp. Dijon mustard
2 bay leaves
½ cup olive oil
1 tbsp. jalapeno pepper sauce
½ lb. crawfish tails

½ bunch green onions, chopped
2 fresh tomatoes, chopped
½ cup white wine
1 oz. Worcestershire sauce
1 tbsp. basil
1 cup flour
½ tsp. chopped garlic
2 tbsp. margarine
1 whole egg
1 pt. milk

Mix milk and egg together with a wire whisk to make egg wash.

Heat oil in sauté pan. Put crabs in egg wash, then in flour, shaking off excess flour. Then put in sauté pan, face down. Brown on both sides. Set aside.

Put garlic in pan, then margarine, tomatoes, sea scallops, crawfish tails, bay leaves, mustard, white wine, Worcestershire sauce, lemon juice, salt, basil, green onions, and jalapeno pepper sauce. Cook on low heat 5-8 minutes, and add the crabs. They are ready to serve. I suggest serving the crabs with Stuffed Tomatoes and Idaho Potatoes Dauphine (see index for recipes).

BROILED SOFT-SHELL CRABS

It was a celebrated New Orleans chef who first decided to broil the soft-shell crab. His success was great and "Crabes à la Créole" were in great demand at once at the hotels and restaurants.

1 dozen soft-shell crabs	1 pt. milk
2 tsp. flour, sifted	Butter
Lemon	Parsley for garnish

Clean the crabs, according to accepted procedure, and wash in cold water. Dry with a clean towel and season and soak the crabs in milk so as to impregnate them thoroughly with the milk. Then pat lightly with a little flour and brush over with melted butter. Place in a slow broiler until a delicate brown. Serve on a platter, nicely garnished with parsley sprigs and lemon cut in quarters. Pour over the crabs a little melted butter and chopped parsley and you will have a famous Creole dish.

FRIED SOFT-SHELL CRAB

6-8 cleaned soft-shell crabs	2 cups all-purpose flour
2 eggs	2 tsp. pepper
1 pt. milk	Oil for frying
1 tbsp. salt	

Mix eggs and milk together. Mix flour, salt, and pepper together. Put the crabs in the egg wash, then in the flour. Shake before putting in oil to fry. Fry crabs at 325° for approximately 4 minutes. When placing the crab in frying pan, do not crowd them. Place them in one at a time, slowly, claws first.

SOFT-SHELL CRAB PO' BOY

Every year, chefs in New Orleans stage a po' boy contest for the most unique variation. New Orleans is famous for this type of sandwich, and La Fête Po' Boy Contest was designed to bring more business into the city. Soft-shell crabs were in season when I created this, but I had only one problem — I ran out of crabs! Anyway, everyone enjoyed it, so I put it on Kabby's menu.

1 cup olive oil
1 tsp. onion salt
1 tsp. garlic, finely chopped
1 tsp. thyme
2 bay leaves
½ tsp. cayenne pepper
1 julienne-cut zucchini
4 fresh mushrooms, sliced
1 French loaf
2 jumbo soft-shell crabs
½ cup melted butter

1 tsp. paprika
1 tsp. jalapeno pepper
  sauce
½ tsp. basil
½ tsp. white pepper
1 tsp. dry mustard
½ tsp. salt
All-purpose flour
½ tsp. mayonnaise
1 tsp. Creole mustard
Juice of 1 lemon

Mix olive oil, onion salt, jalapeno pepper sauce, paprika, bay leaves, garlic, thyme, basil, lemon juice, cayenne, white pepper, dry mustard, and salt. Place soft-shell crabs in it. Let set for 45 minutes to 1 hour, then dust in flour. Sauté with butter until brown. Set aside. Then sauté the zucchini and the sliced mushrooms in same pan for 5-8 minutes. Toast the French loaf. Cut in half. Mix mayonnaise and Creole mustard together and spread on French loaf. Place crabs on loaf. Add zucchini and mushrooms. Put top of bread on and serve.

LINGUINE CRAB CAKES

Crab cakes are popular at many restaurants. Most places fry them. Some places even substitute crawfish for crabmeat.

I came up with this recipe after cooking Linguine for a special one day. I had some left over — enough to serve again. There was no one in my little kitchen but me, so I chopped some seasoning and added crabmeat. It looked and tasted so good that I let some of my cooks taste it, and they loved it. The next year I was at Kabby's in the Hilton. I would run a special on the crab cakes and serve them with Creole sauce.

½ rib celery, finely chopped
¼ bunch green onions, finely chopped
½ tsp. thyme
1 clove garlic, finely chopped
1 lb. dark crabmeat
2 bay leaves
¼ lb. margarine
1 egg
½ tsp. basil
½ tsp. cayenne pepper
1 tsp. jalapeno pepper sauce
¼ lb. cooked linguine
½ cup mixed bread crumbs
¼ bell pepper, finely chopped
2 cups seafood stock
Additional bread crumbs

In a sauté pan, place margarine and garlic. Cook 2 minutes. Add celery, bell pepper, and onions. Cook 5 minutes. Add crabmeat. Mix well. Add seafood stock, bay leaves, thyme, basil, cayenne pepper, and jalapeno pepper sauce. Cook for 3 minutes more. Add cooked linguine. Beat in whole egg. Mix well. Add bread crumbs. Let cool. Scoop out each cake about the size of a golf ball. Roll in extra bread crumbs, and sauté in a flat pan until brown on both sides. Yum yum! Serves 4.

CRABMEAT AND EGGPLANT WITH PASTA

1 medium eggplant, peeled
  and cut in ⅛" cubes
4 cups chicken stock
4 cups heavy cream
2 cloves garlic, finely
  chopped
2 oz. margarine
1 lb. crabmeat
½ medium red bell pepper,
  finely chopped

1 tbsp. basil
3 bay leaves
½ cup olive oil
1 oz. green pepper sauce
2 tbsp. all-purpose flour
½ bunch green onions,
  finely chopped
½ oz. Worcestershire
1 lb. cooked pasta

Heat olive oil and margarine in pot. Add garlic and eggplant. Cook for 5 minutes. Add red bell pepper and green onions. Mix well. Stir in flour. Add chicken stock, cream, green pepper sauce, Worcestershire sauce, bay leaves, and basil. Cook on low heat for 10 minutes. Add crabmeat. Cook for an additional 5-8 minutes. Serve over pasta. Serves 4-6.

CRABMEAT AU GRATIN

16 oz. crabmeat
1 pt. milk, heated
4 oz. sherry
4 oz. butter

2 oz. flour
1½ oz. Parmesan cheese
1 tsp. salt

Melt butter in saucepan. Add flour and mix well; do not brown. Add hot milk to this roux and stir constantly. Cook for about 5-8 minutes on low heat. Add salt, sherry, and fold in crabmeat. Place mixture into casserole dish and sprinkle Parmesan cheese over top. Bake in 375° oven till cheese is browned. Serves 3.

STUFFED CRABS

Stuffed crab is a favorite New Orleans and Creole dish. The stuffing is mounded on an actual crab shell. I use soaked French bread instead of bread crumbs. You will get a better flavor when you use claw crabmeat. I use lump crabmeat because I don't like biting into the shell.

1 lb. lump crabmeat
2 hard French loaves
8 eggs
½ bunch green onions,
  chopped
½ bell pepper
2 bay leaves

½ clove garlic, chopped
½ tsp. cayenne pepper
1 lb. butter
1 rib celery, chopped
½ bunch parsley
1 lb. bread crumbs

Soak hard French loaves in cold water. Place ½ pound of butter in sauté pan with garlic, celery, bell pepper, bay leaves, cayenne, parsley, and green onions. Cook until vegetables are tender. Add the soaked French bread, crabmeat, and eggs. Mix well. Place in a baking pan in the oven at 450° for 30 minutes, then stuff in crab shells and sprinkle with bread crumbs and butter. Return to oven until brown. Serves 4.

CRABMEAT AND OYSTERS AU GRATIN

1 lb. crabmeat
2 tbsp. butter
1 tbsp. bell pepper, chopped
Cream
Salt

1 qt. oysters
½ onion, grated
2 tbsp. flour
Lemon juice
Buttered bread crumbs

Cook oysters in their liquid until edges curl; strain, reserving liquid. Sauté onion and bell pepper lightly in butter. Add flour, oyster liquid, and enough cream to make a thick sauce. Season with salt and lemon juice; add oysters and crabmeat. Place in a baking dish, sprinkle with buttered crumbs, and bake in 350° oven for 5-10 minutes until heated. Serves 2.

CRABMEAT EN COQUILLE

2 lb. crabmeat	½ cup bread crumbs
1 cup Cream Sauce	1 tbsp. dry mustard
(see below)	½ cup Hollandaise Sauce

Preheat oven to 450°. Blend Cream Sauce, Hollandaise Sauce, and mustard together. Add crabmeat and then place in coquille shells. Sprinkle bread crumbs over the crabmeat. Bake in oven for 15 minutes and serve. Serves 6.

CREAM SAUCE

¼ lb. butter	2 tbsp. flour
2 cups milk, heated	Dash salt
1 cup water	1 egg yolk

Melt butter in saucepan. Add flour and cook for 3 minutes. Add hot milk and salt. Cook for 10 minutes on medium heat. Beat egg yolk and water together. Stir into sauce constantly. Cook sauce for another 3 minutes and turn off heat.

CRAB LOUIS

1 cup mayonnaise	Salt and freshly ground
⅓ cup French dressing	black pepper
¼ cup chili sauce	Chilled lettuce, torn into
2 tbsp. minced chives	bite-sized pieces
2 tbsp. minced green olives	3 cups cooked crabmeat,
1 tsp. horseradish	flaked
4 hard-boiled eggs, cut in	1 tsp. Worcestershire sauce
quarters	Capers
Quartered tomatoes	

Combine the mayonnaise, French dressing, chili sauce, chives, olives, and seasonings. Chill. Arrange the lettuce in a shallow, chilled salad bowl and mound the crabmeat on top. Spoon the dressing on top and garnish with hard-boiled egg, tomato quarters, and capers. Serves 3.

CRABMEAT SAUTE ROYALE

4 oz. butter	½ bunch green onions,
Juice of 1 lemon	chopped
¼ tsp. white pepper	1 lb. lump crabmeat
Salt	1 oz. Worcestershire sauce

In a sauté pan, combine butter, crabmeat, green onions, pepper, and lemon juice. Add just a pinch of salt, then the Worcestershire sauce, and mix well. You don't have to cook this dish long because the crabmeat is already cooked — no longer than 10 minutes. Serve with Almond Rice. Serves 2.

ALMOND RICE

1 cup cooked rice	2 tsp. sliced cooked
1 tsp. butter	almonds
¼ tsp. white pepper	¼ cup green peas, cooked

In sauté pan, place butter, rice, and green peas. Mix well. Add white pepper, sliced cooked almonds, and cook for 8-10 minutes. Serve.

OYSTERS AND ARTICHOKES
WITH FRESH HERBS

If you have fresh herbs, and plenty of them, your dishes have a good start. When I created this dish in the fall, it didn't take long to make. The oysters were fresh, so it was easy. All I needed was to get a light wine to enhance the flavor, and the best wine is a dry Vermouth. I serve this dish at Kabby's in the Hilton.

2 pt. oysters with water	**¼ tsp. dill, chopped**
2 cups heavy cream	**1 bunch green onions,**
1 tbsp. chopped parsley	**chopped**
8 medium mushrooms,	**2 oz. green pepper sauce**
sliced	**8 hearts of artichoke, cut**
1 cup Vermouth	**4 oz. butter**
1 tbsp. salt	**3 oz. flour**
¼ tsp. rosemary	**2 bay leaves**
¼ tsp. basil, chopped	**1 qt. chicken stock**

Place oysters in pot with chicken stock, bay leaves, and herbs. Let come to a boil. Skim off the top. In another pot, melt butter. Add sliced mushrooms and cook for 3-4 minutes. Add flour and green onions; mix well. Add oysters and liquid and mix well. Add Vermouth, heavy cream, green pepper sauce, salt, and cut-up artichoke hearts. Cook for 15 minutes more on low heat. Serve over pasta. Serves 4.

BAKED OYSTERS IN STILL CHAMPAGNE

In a small saucepan reduce 1½ cups Coteaux Champenois or other dry white wine with 1 tbsp. minced shallot over high heat to ¼ cup. Add ½ cup Crème Fraîche (see below) and reduce the mixture over high heat to ¼ cup. Add ½ cup Crème Fraîche and reduce the mixture over moderate heat to ½ cup. In a small bowl whisk 2 tbsp. of the sauce into 1 egg yolk, lightly beaten. Stir the mixture into the remaining sauce, and heat the sauce over low heat until it thickens. Do not let it boil. Add salt and pepper to taste and remove the pan from the heat. Shuck 12 oysters, leaving them on the half-shell, and sprinkle them with pepper. Arrange the oysters on a bed of coarse salt (to keep them from tipping) in a gratin dish and bake them in a preheated hot oven (450°) for 3 minutes. Divide the sauce among the oysters and put the dish under a preheated broiler about 2 inches from the heat for 15 seconds, or until the tops are glazed. Serves 2 or 3.

CREME FRAICHE

In a jar combine 1 cup heavy cream and 2½ tsp. buttermilk. Cover the jar tightly and shake the mixture for at least 1 minute. Let the cream set at room temperature for at least 8 hours, or until it is thick. Store it, covered, in the refrigerator. Keeps 4 to 6 weeks. Makes about 1 cup.

OYSTER AND ARTICHOKE CASSEROLE

8 large artichokes
1½ cups (2½ sticks) butter
3 tbsp. chopped green
  onions
2 tsp. salt
1 can (7 oz.) mushroom
  pieces

2½ dozen oysters in liquid
3 tbsp. flour
Bread crumbs
2 oz. Pernod
Salt and pepper

Steam artichokes in boiling salted water until tender, about 45 minutes. Drain and cool slightly. Scrape meat from leaves and cut hearts in half. Stir flour in heated skillet over low heat until light brown. Set aside. Melt butter, add green onions, and sauté about 5 minutes. Add flour to butter mixture and stir until smooth. Mix in remaining ingredients, except bread crumbs. Place in casserole, cover with bread crumbs, and bake in oven at 350° for 15 minutes. Serves 6.

OYSTERS EN BROCHETTE

½ lb. bacon strips, cut into
  2" lengths
3 dozen fresh, select oysters
2 cups flour

4-6 tbsp. solid shortening
½ tomato, broiled
Parsley
Lemon slice

In a skillet, fry bacon until transparent, but not crisp. Remove and drain. On a 10-inch skewer, alternate pieces of bacon and oysters, using approximately 9 oysters per skewer. Dredge skewered oysters and bacon in flour until well coated. Shake off excess flour and sauté in shortening until crisp on the outside and golden brown. Remove from sauté pan; slide skewer out. Garnish with half-broiled tomato, parsley, and slice of lemon.

GRILLED OYSTER LOAF

This is a new twist on a popular local standard. Grilled Oyster Loaf is slathered with fried mirlitons and a spicy dressing. I entered it in the 1989 La Fête Po' Boy Contest. Here's the recipe.

2 dozen drained oysters
  (save water)
¼ stick butter
½ tsp. flour
French bread, toasted
2 large (Creole) tomatoes,
  sliced
1 whole pickle, sliced
2 bay leaves

½ tsp. oregano
1 tsp. jalapeno green
  pepper sauce
2 medium mirlitons, peeled
1 egg
1 pt. milk
1½ cups Italian bread
  crumbs

Drain oysters. Cook them on a flat-top grill, or in heavy iron skillet until oysters brown on both sides. Remove from pan. Scrape pan out. In same pan, place butter and flour, mixing well, until half-brown. Then add water from drained oysters and bay leaves and mix well. Add oregano and jalapeno green pepper sauce; mix well. Add oysters. Split the loaves of toasted French bread. Place oysters on the bread. Slice mirlitons ⅛" thick. Steam lightly for 5 minutes, and drain.

Mix egg with milk. Add mirlitons. Dredge in Italian bread crumbs. Fry till brown.

Place on brown paper to drain. Place mirlitons on loaf with oysters. Top with Creole tomatoes and pickle. Serve and enjoy. Serves 2.

OYSTER PATTIE

1 tsp. oregano leaves
¼ lb. butter
6 chicken bouillon cubes
1 tsp. cayenne pepper
1 oz. green pepper sauce
2 pt. oysters, chopped
3 bay leaves
4 cups oyster water
3 oz. all-purpose flour

1 rib celery, chopped
Parmesan cheese
¼ cup half & half cream
½ bunch green onions,
   chopped
1 tsp. chopped garlic
2 eggs
36 pattie shells

Sauté celery, green onions, and garlic in butter for 3-4 minutes. Add flour; mix well. In another pot put the oysters in water. Let come to a boil. Skim off top. Add bay leaves, oregano leaves, chicken cubes, cayenne pepper, and green pepper sauce. Then add the oyster mix to the flour. Mix well. Turn heat to low; let cook for 15-20 minutes. Mix the eggs and cream together and stir in. Mix well. Let cook for 5-8 minutes more. Let cool and stuff into pattie shells. Sprinkle grated cheese on top of pattie shells.

OYSTERS EVANS

At Kabby's we use plenty of oysters. We have an Oyster Bar, and offer them for brunch. We serve them with pasta, fried, grilled, or any way you want them. This recipe, Oysters Evans, was created for Sunday Brunch. I wanted to have a dish that no one else had and it turned out that this was unique. My guests always ask for the recipe and say they never tasted anything like it.

½ gallon oysters
1 tsp. oregano
3 oz. flour
½ lb. butter
½ tsp. caramel color
1 pt. cream
3 bay leaves

1 oz. Worcestershire sauce
1 qt. oyster water
½ tsp. cayenne pepper
2 oz. chicken base
1 oz. green pepper sauce
1 bunch green onions, chopped

Drain oysters. Save water. Cook oysters in heavy saucepan. Scrape the crust from pan. Make sure heavy pan is very hot before putting in oysters. Remove oysters and set aside. Add butter to pan and melt. Add flour. Mix well. In another pot, put the oyster water in. Bring to a boil. Skim off the top, adding it to the flour and butter. Mix well. Add all remaining ingredients, except the oysters, mixing well. Let cook for 10 minutes. Then add oysters and cook for 5 minutes. Serve and enjoy. Serves 10.

OYSTERS BURGUNDY

6 oysters
½ tbsp. butter
1 tbsp. green onion, chopped
Salt and pepper

½ tsp. lemon juice
½ tsp. parsley, chopped
½ tsp. garlic, minced
Bread crumbs

Open 6 to 8 oysters for each serving and leave them in the deep side of the shell. Place these on a bed of rock salt in a rather shallow tin plate. Cream butter with green onions, using mostly the green part, parsley, and garlic. Add salt and pepper to taste and lemon juice. Cover each oyster with this paste, about the size of a hazelnut. Top with bread crumbs and bake in moderately hot oven for about 10 minutes, or until crumbs brown. Do not overbake. Serve immediately. Serves 1.

OYSTER PAN ROAST

8 freshly opened oysters	2 tbsp. (¼ stick) butter
1 tbsp. chili sauce	1 tsp. Worcestershire sauce
¼ cup oyster liquor	½ tsp. paprika
Dash celery salt	½ cup cream
Dash dry white wine	1 slice dry toast

Place all ingredients except cream, toast, paprika, and 1 tbsp. of the butter in the top part of a double boiler over boiling water. Don't let the top pan touch the water. Whisk or stir briskly and constantly for about 1 minute, until oysters are just beginning to curl. Add cream and continue stirring briskly, just to a boil. *Do not boil.* Pour pan roast into a soup plate over the slice of dry toast. Top with remaining 1 tbsp. butter, and sprinkle with paprika.

Even though the oysters are the most popular, my Oyster Bar serves other individual stews and pan roasts that can be made at home in your own kitchen. In each recipe, simply substitute the following for the oysters. *Shrimp:* Use 8 or 9 raw shrimp, shelled, deveined, and with tails off. *Clams:* Use 8 or 9 freshly opened cherrystone or littleneck clams. *Lobster:* Use ¼ lb. fresh lobster meat. *Scallops:* Use 10 or 12 raw bay scallops. *Mussel Stew:* Use 14 or 15 freshly opened mussels, bearded and in the shell. Serves 2.

OYSTERS CASINO

24 oysters on the half-shell	½ cup butter
⅓ cup chopped shallots	¼ cup chopped parsley
¼ cup chopped bell pepper	Lemon juice
Bacon, partially cooked	

Arrange the oysters, in their shells, on beds of rock salt. Blend together the butter, shallots, parsley, and bell pepper. Spoon this over the oysters and add a dash of lemon juice to each one. Top with pieces of partially cooked bacon. Bake in a 450° oven until the bacon is brown and the oysters are cooked through.

OYSTERS A LA POULETTE

24 freshly opened oysters
2 tbsp. butter
1 pt. rich cream
Celery salt
1 small white onion
1 tbsp. Worcestershire sauce
Hot buttered toast

½ tsp. paprika
1 tsp. minced parsley
Dash mace
½ cup sliced mushrooms
3 oz. dry white wine
2 egg yolks

Drain oysters. In a chafing dish melt 1 tbsp. butter. Add to it cream, lightly beaten, the juice of 1 small peeled white onion, celery salt to taste, Worcestershire sauce, ¼ tsp. paprika, parsley, mace, ¼ cup sliced fresh mushrooms which have been sautéed in 1 tbsp. of butter until tender, and dry American white wine. Allow this mixture to come just to the boiling point. Add the whole oysters and poach gently until the edges begin to curl. Then stir in 2 lightly beaten egg yolks, and cook over low heat until the mixture thickens. Check for additional seasoning, and pour over slice of hot buttered toast, serving immediately. Serves 3.

OYSTERS ODETTE

3 dozen large or small
  oysters
1 medium white onion
1 large piece celery,
  finely chopped
1 heaping tsp. butter
1 tsp. yellow prepared
  mustard

1 cup bread crumbs
Dash thyme
Slice of lemon for garnish
½ cup chopped mushrooms
2 tsp. dry mustard
1 egg

Sauté onion and celery together in butter. Chop oysters and add to sautéed onion and celery. Add bread crumbs. Add remaining ingredients and cook for 15 minutes. Fill oyster shells. Bake in oven at 450° for 20 minutes. Serves 4.

BREADED SCALLOPS

32 bay scallops or 16 ocean
  scallops
Salt and freshly ground
  pepper
Flour for dredging
1 large or 2 small eggs,
  lightly beaten

1½ cups fresh bread
  crumbs
Fat for deep frying
Lemon wedges and parsley,
  for garnish
Tartar sauce

If bay scallops are used, leave them whole; if ocean scallops are used, cut them in half. Season scallops with salt and pepper. Dredge them in flour and coat with egg. Dredge them in bread crumbs and deep fry for 2 to 3 minutes at 360° (depending on size). Garnish with lemon wedges and parsley and serve with tartar sauce. Serves 4.

Poultry and Game

I guess chicken is more versatile than any other entree. Game is gaining in popularity each year. There are 365 days in a year, so we have to find something to eat, and if we eat three meals a day we want something different. But chicken we seem to come back to often.

Sometimes I bake chicken. When I worked for the Pontchartrain, the owner, Mr. Albert, liked a half-chicken baked in an orange glaze. This has currant jelly in it, along with orange juice. He ate chicken about three or four times a day.

One of the oldest chicken dishes that I know of is Chicken Fricassee. I have seen it fixed in a cream sauce. I am told that was the French way, but we Creoles use a brown sauce.

This section is packed with good recipes, from Chicken Cordon Bleu, to Stewed Rabbit à la Créole (with no wine), to the ever-popular Rock Cornish hens. Give these a try, and enjoy the results!

ORANGE-GLAZED CHICKEN

1 whole fryer cut in half
  (2½-3 lb.)
1 cup brown sauce
1 cup orange juice

2 oz. Grand Marnier liqueur
½ fresh orange, sliced
2 tsp. red currant jelly

In a pot, combine brown sauce, orange juice, red currant jelly, and liqueur. Bring to a boil and reduce heat. Take the fryer, which has been washed and dried, place on a flat pan, put in oven at 350° for 25 minutes, and drain off grease. Baste with the brown sauce mix occasionally as it continues cooking for 15 minutes. Place one slice of orange on each chicken half, and cook for 10 minutes more. Serves 2.

STEWED CHICKEN

1 large fryer
Salt and pepper to taste
2 tbsp. shortening
2 tbsp. flour
2 medium onions, finely
  chopped

2 ribs celery, finely chopped
½ bell pepper, chopped
½ bunch green onions,
  finely chopped
1 bay leaf
3 cups water

Cut chicken into serving pieces. Salt and pepper to taste and place in a large saucepan. Melt shortening in skillet; add flour and brown well. Add onions and cook for 5 minutes. Add water, stir well, then add celery, bell pepper, green onions, and bay leaf. Pour this mixture over the chicken, which you have browned. Cook for 45 minutes or until tender. Stir from bottom frequently to prevent sticking. Serve with steamed rice. Serves 3.

CHICKEN MACINTOSH

This dish was created for the St. Michael's Special School annual charity event. Every year for St. Michael's, each chef has to prepare a new dish. This is more of a holiday entree because of the apple and the water chestnuts. It is a lunch special at Kabby's, in the Hilton. This dish can be served with pasta or white rice.

3 boneless 8-oz. chicken
  breasts (reserve bones)
1 tsp. thyme
1 bay leaf
½ tsp. salt
¼ tsp. pepper
¼ cup shortening
8 oz. water chestnuts
1 white onion (½ chopped,
  ½ sliced)

1 rib celery, chopped
1 carrot, chopped
½ bell pepper, chopped
6 oz. flour
1½ qt. chicken stock
2 cups white wine
1 large red apple, unpeeled
  and cut in quarters
1 tbsp. butter

Salt and pepper chicken (save remaining salt and pepper). Dust in 2 oz. flour. Place in shortening with skin toward bottom of pan and brown on both sides.

Remove chicken from sauté pan. Add 4 oz. flour and stir into shortening left in pan. Cook until browned. Add chopped onion, chopped celery, chopped bell pepper, chopped carrot, thyme, bay leaf, balance of salt and pepper, and bones from chicken. Cook for about 15 minutes on low heat. Reduce to half.

Add chicken stock and cook for about 30 minutes. Remove bones.

In another pan, add sliced onion and butter. Cook for about 5 minutes. Place chicken breasts in this pan. Add water chestnuts and apple quarters. Add wine and cook for another 5 minutes.

Add stock and strain over chicken breasts. Place in oven for about 15-20 minutes at 350° and serve with rice. Serves 3.

CHICKEN SAUTE WITH TOMATOES

2½-3 lb. chicken
1 small onion, chopped
1 tbsp. flour
4 tomatoes, peeled, seeded, and chopped
1 tsp. chopped parsley
Salt and pepper

2 tbsp. butter or oil
½ glass white wine
½ cup stock or leftover gravy
4 baked stuffed tomatoes for garnish

Clean chicken and cut for sautéing. Season pieces with salt and pepper. Put butter or oil in saucepan and cook until golden brown on all sides. Add chopped onion and continue cooking slowly until golden brown. Sprinkle in the flour; add wine and stock. Cover pan and cook 25-30 minutes. Remove chicken to another pan and then strain sauce over it. Add fresh chopped tomatoes and cook about 15 minutes longer. Put in serving dish, garnish with stuffed tomatoes, and sprinkle with parsley. Serves 3-4.

CHICKEN STOCK

3 lb. chicken necks
1 medium yellow onion, chopped
2 ribs celery, chopped

6 qt. water
3 lb. chicken backs
1½ cups carrots, chopped
2 bay leaves

Put all ingredients above in a pot. Let boil. Skim off the top and reduce to simmer. Let cook until you have 2 quarts. Take off heat and strain.

Suggestion: Chicken stock can be made with hen—the stock will be stronger. If you are going to save some of the stock, leave the fat on until you are ready to use.

CHICKEN MARENGO

1 frying chicken (2-3 lb.)
⅓ cup flour
¼ tsp. pepper
1 tsp. salt
¼ cup olive oil
1 clove garlic, crushed
4 tomatoes, cut in quarters
3 tbsp. chopped onion

1 cup white wine
Herb Bouquet (see below)
2 tbsp. butter
1 cup sliced mushrooms
½ cup sliced olives
½ cup cold Consommé
(see below)
2 tbsp. flour

Clean chicken, which should weigh 2-3 lb. when it's ready to cook. Disjoint and cut into serving-size pieces. Rinse and pat dry with absorbent paper. To coat chicken evenly, shake 2 or 3 pieces at a time in a plastic bag containing a mixture of the ⅓ cup flour, pepper, and salt.

Heat olive oil in a large, heavy skillet which has a tight-fitting cover. Brown chicken in the hot oil. Add garlic, tomatoes, onion, wine, and Herb Bouquet. Cover and simmer over low heat about ½ hour, or until thickest pieces of chicken are tender when pierced with a fork.

Put butter in a small skillet and sauté mushrooms. Add to chicken with olives. To thicken liquid, put into a screw-top jar and add ½ cup Consommé. Sprinkle 2 tbsp. flour over it. Cover and shake well.

Remove chicken from skillet and discard Herb Bouquet. Gradually add Consommé-flour liquid to mixture in skillet, stirring constantly. Boil 3 to 5 minutes until mixture thickens. Return chicken to sauce, cover, and simmer 10 minutes. Arrange chicken on a hot platter. Cover with the sauce. Serves 4-5.

Note: If poultry is frozen, thaw according to directions on package.

HERB BOUQUET

3-4 sprigs parsley   **½ bay leaf**
1 sprig thyme

Tie herbs neatly together. If fine, dry herbs must be used, enclose in a cheesecloth bag. A bouquet of aromatic herbs is commonly used to flavor soups, stews, braised dishes, and sauces.

CONSOMME

This is a clear, concentrated stock or broth usually made from a combination of two or more kinds of meat, such as beef, veal, and poultry. Season it strongly, strain it, and clarify it. A quick substitute is 1 chicken bouillon cube dissolved in 1 cup hot water.

CHICKEN SAUTE WITH FINE CHAMPAGNE BRANDY

2 frying chickens, 2½ lb.   **⅙ pt. sweet cream**
each, cut in parts   **3½ oz. raw sliced truffles**
Butter   **1 tsp. chopped shallots**
½ oz. fine champagne   **Lemon juice**
1½ oz. brandy

Sauté chicken parts in butter until light brown. Add truffles and shallots and cook for 3 more minutes. Remove the chicken only and place in a casserole dish. Place saucepan with the truffles and shallots on the heat again. Swirl into it a mixture of the champagne and brandy. Add the lemon juice and sweet cream. Pour over chicken. Taste and say, *"Magnifique!"* Serves 6.

CHICKEN MARCO POLO

1 boneless 7-oz. chicken
  breast
3 oz. butter or margarine
1 slice (3 oz.) ham
4 oz. broccoli

Red or purple grapes for
  garnish
3 oz. Poulette Sauce (see
  below)

Pound chicken breast with a mallet. Sauté chicken breast 2 to 3 minutes on both sides in the butter or margarine. Remove chicken from pan. Grill ham on both sides 1 to 2 minutes. Steam the broccoli 2 to 3 minutes. To assemble this dish, place ham on the plate first. Place chicken breast on top of grilled ham. Place broccoli on each side of chicken breast. Garnish with red or purple grapes. Top with Poulette Sauce. Serves 1.

POULETTE SAUCE

3 lb. chicken bones
4 cups water
Salt and pepper
1 cup heavy cream

2 oz. flour
1½ oz. butter or margarine
4 oz. cheddar cheese,
  grated

Make chicken stock by boiling chicken bones in the water. Reduce to 2 cups. Salt and pepper to taste, then add cream. Bring to boil again.

Cook flour in the butter or margarine to make a roux. Thicken the boiling sauce with the roux, stirring sauce constantly with wire whisk. Add cheese and continue to stir with whisk on low heat until cheese melts.

CHICKEN CHOW MEIN

3 lb. fryer or roaster
  chicken
½ cup chicken stock
⅓ cup peanut oil
½ lb. mushrooms
1 cup Pascal celery, cut in
  very narrow strips (about
  3" long)
1 cup bok choy, cut the same

1 cup snow pea pods,
  halved diagonally
½ cup sliced water chestnuts
2 cups fresh bean sprouts
2 tsp. salt
⅛ tsp. Oriental dark
  seasoning
½ tsp. garlic salt
2 tbsp. cornstarch

Debone chicken and cut meat in 3-inch-long, very flat strips, about ¼ inch wide. Dark and white meat of chicken may be used. This should make 2 cups raw chicken. With bones, gizzard, etc., prepare chicken stock. In a large deep skillet, heat peanut oil. Add chicken strips and sauté for several minutes, turning continuously to prevent browning. Cover and steam chicken about 7 to 8 minutes over medium heat.

Slice the mushrooms medium-thick. Add them with all the other vegetables to chicken. Continue to cook over medium heat, uncovered, for about 5 minutes, mixing with 2 forks as it cooks. Sprinkle with salt, Oriental dark seasoning, and garlic salt. Cook for about 2 minutes more, turning often.

Add chicken stock mixed with cornstarch. Cover and cook until thick and glazy—about 5 or 6 minutes—turning gently as it cooks. If too thick, add more stock. If it does not appear glazy after it simmers several minutes, add a little more peanut oil and continue to cook for another 1 or 2 minutes. Serves 3.

ROAST CHICKEN FOR TWO

Giblets
2½ lb. whole broiler fryer
½ tsp. salt
¼ cup butter or margarine
¼ cup finely chopped onion
¼ cup water
1 cup packaged herb-
  seasoned stuffing
2 tbsp. soft butter or
  margarine

Paprika
1 tsp. instant minced onion
¼ tsp. salt
1 cup cut carrots
1 cup cut celery
2 cups water
1 chicken liver
1 chicken bouillon cube
2 tbsp. flour

Preheat oven to 325°. Remove giblets and necks from chicken; set aside to make chicken broth for gravy if desired. Wash and dry chicken inside and out. Rub inside with the ½ tsp. salt.

To make the stuffing, heat the ¼ cup butter in medium skillet and cook chopped onion until tender—about 5 minutes. Add the ¼ cup water and packaged stuffing, fluffing up with a fork.

When stuffing is done, lightly fill body cavity of chicken with it. Bring skin over neck opening; fasten to back with poultry pin. Close body cavity with pins. Pin wings to body, then tie legs together at ends with twine. Place chicken on rack, breast side down, in shallow, open roasting pan. Brush with 1 tbsp. of the soft butter. Roast uncovered for 45 minutes.

Turn chicken breast side up. Brush with remaining butter; sprinkle with paprika. Roast 1¼ hours longer or until leg moves freely when twisted and fleshy part of drumstick feels soft. Remove chicken to warm serving platter; remove pins and twine; keep warm.

To make chicken broth for gravy, combine giblets, instant onion, the ¼ tsp. salt, carrots, celery, and the 2 cups water in a small saucepan. Bring to boiling. Reduce heat; simmer, covered, for 1 hour and 45 minutes. Add liver and bouillon cube. Simmer 15 minutes longer. Strain broth, pressing vegetables through sieve along with broth.

To make gravy, add flour to pan drippings, stirring to make a smooth mixture. Gradually add 1 cup chicken broth, stirring until smooth. Bring to boiling over direct heat. Reduce heat; simmer 1 minute.

To serve chicken, cut in half lengthwise with poultry shears through backbone and breastbone. Serve gravy hot along with chicken.

CHICKEN SMOTHERED WITH ITALIAN MUSHROOMS

2 2½-lb. fryers	**¼ lb. butter**
½ cup flour	**2 shallots**
½ tsp. salt	**½ cup dried Italian**
1 tsp. black pepper	**mushrooms**

First have your butcher cut the 2 chickens into quarters. Ask to remove the spinal cord and neck as well as the rib bone behind the breast. Put flour, salt and black pepper in a brown paper bag. Put the chicken pieces in the bag and shake back and forth, up and down, until all the pieces are well coated.

Melt butter in a heavy iron skillet (be sure it has a cover). Mince shallots very, very fine. Put in butter and cook until tender. *Important:* Keep heat low and do not allow butter to brown. Put the chicken in the butter, cover, and cook 15 minutes over medium heat. While chicken is cooking put dried Italian mushrooms in a measuring cup and fill to top with boiling water. Allow to soak for 15 minutes.

Pour drained mushroom water over chicken to make gravy. Reserve mushrooms. Cover skillet and cook another 15 minutes. At the end of cooking time remove the chicken to hot platter. Add the mushrooms to the gravy. Turn heat high and stir for exactly 2 minutes. Return chicken to gravy and serve directly out of skillet or pour gravy over chicken on hot platter. Serves 6.

ALFRED'S CHICKEN

2 2½ lb. fryers
2 large onions, minced
2 tbsp. lemon juice
2 heaping tbsp. parsley,
   minced
Salt and pepper

Chopped parsley
½ lb. butter
1 lb. fresh mushrooms
   (stems on)
1 cup good sherry wine, dry

Preheat broiler to medium. Cut fryers into quarters. Melt ¼ lb. butter slowly. Smear the chicken with butter. Set chicken pieces in the broiler pan (not on grill) and brown for about 5-8 minutes on each side until a deep rich brown. Remove from broiler. The chicken at this point should not be quite done through. It will be cooked more later on. Set aside in a good-sized casserole. Preheat oven to 350°.

You may start this sauce while the chicken is broiling. Melt remaining butter in skillet and add onions. Cover and cook until golden and almost mushy but never allow to brown. Add sliced mushrooms with stems on, using the brown "beefsteak" variety if possible. Cover and cook slowly until mushrooms are limp. Stir occasionally during cooking.

Add lemon juice, parsley, and sherry, being very sure *not* to use dessert sherry. Simmer very slowly, well covered, for 10 minutes. Season to taste with salt and pepper and pour the sauce over the chicken. Put the casserole in a preheated 350° oven and cook for 30 minutes until glazed, hot, and cooked through. During the baking period baste several times, especially being sure to baste at least once the last 5 minutes. Serve with little browned potato balls around the edge of the casserole. Garnish with chopped parsley. Serves 6.

BROILED CHICKEN

2½-3 lb. chicken, in 24
   pieces
1 cup flour
2 level tsp. pepper
White wine

Water
¾ lb. butter
1⅓ heaping tbsp. salt
½ cup tarragon tea
Crisco

In stone jar, marinate chicken pieces in equal parts wine and water, and ½ cup tarragon tea, for 24 hours.

In plastic bag, shake chicken in flour, salt, and pepper, and shake well so that the pieces are well covered. Place the 24 pieces of chicken on 2 broiler racks (the folding racks) which have been greased with Crisco. Place the racks over hot charcoal fire about 20 inches over fire. (If they are not cooking fast enough and do not blacken at all, move done somewhat.) The cooking should take about 30 minutes. When done, stand broiler on an end and pour melted butter over several times to cover chicken. Remove and serve.

CHICKEN CORDON BLEU

4 8-oz. chicken breasts,
   boneless
4 thin slices ham

8 thin slices Swiss cheese
12 mushrooms, sliced
¼ cup butter

Melt butter. Put chicken on flat pan, put butter over it, and bake in oven at 350° for 20 minutes. Take out. Cook ham in sauté pan; do not brown. Then put the mushrooms in same pan. Place 1 slice of ham under each chicken breast and put the sliced mushrooms on top of each breast. Cover with Swiss cheese and put back in oven for 5 more minutes or until cheese melts and serve. Serves 4.

SAUTEED CHICKEN BERCY

Prepare a 2½-3 lb. chicken for sautéing. In a skillet melt 3 tbsp. butter and arrange the pieces of chicken skin down on it. Cook the chicken over medium heat until the skin is golden brown. Remove the breast meat to a hot serving platter and cook the remaining pieces for 5 to 10 minutes longer, or until they are tender. Remove the remaining pieces to the platter. To the juices in the pan add 1 tbsp. finely chopped shallots or onion and 1 tsp. flour. Stir in ¼ cup white wine, ¼ cup chicken broth, and 3 tbsp. tomato sauce. Cook the sauce for a few minutes, stirring, until it is slightly thickened. Correct the seasoning. Return the chicken to the pan and simmer it for about 5 minutes. Arrange the chicken on the serving platter, strain the sauce around it, and sprinkle with chopped parsley. Serves 4.

SAUTEED CHICKEN FLORENTINE

Prepare Sautéed Chicken Bercy. Sauté 1½ lb. well-cleaned, cooked, and drained spinach in 2 tbsp. butter for 3 to 4 minutes. Make a bed of the spinach on a serving platter and arrange the chicken on it with cooked, sliced mushrooms or pieces for foie gras and slices of truffle on top. Pour the sauce over all. Serves 4.

CHICKEN IN CHAMPAGNE
SAUCE

2 3½-4 lb. broiler-fryer
   chickens, cut into 8 pieces
10 tbsp. unsalted butter
2 tbsp. olive oil
1¼ brut champagne
1 cup chicken stock
½ tsp. salt

½ tsp. freshly ground
   pepper
3 large shallots, minced
   (about ⅓ cup)
1 cup Crème Fraîche
½ lb. mushrooms, quartered
   and sautéed (optional)

Preheat the oven to 375°. Pat the chicken dry with paper towels. Season all over with salt and pepper. In a large, heavy ovenproof skillet, melt 4 tbsp. of the butter in the olive oil over moderate heat. When the foam begins to subside, add the chicken and sauté, turning once, until golden, about 5 minutes a side. Remove the chicken and set aside.

Add the shallots to the skillet, reduce the heat to moderately low, and sauté, shaking the pan frequently, until just softened, about 1 minute. Return the chicken to the pan and stir to coat with the shallot butter. Pour the chicken, shallots, and butter into a colander, let drain for 2-3 minutes to remove excess fat, and return to the skillet.

Add the champagne and bring to a boil over moderate heat. Cook for 2 minutes; turn the chicken and partially cover the skillet. Boil until the champagne is reduced by half, about 5 minutes. Add the stock, bring to a boil, and cover tightly. Transfer the skillet to the oven and bake until the chicken is tender and its juices run clear when pierced with a fork, about 10 minutes. Remove the chicken to a platter and cover loosely with foil to keep warm. Add the Crème Fraîche to the skillet and boil over moderate heat until the sauce is thick enough to coat a spoon lightly, 15-20 minutes.

Reduce the heat to low. Gradually whisk in the remaining 6 tbsp. butter, 1 or 2 tablespoons at a time, until the sauce is smooth and thickened. Season with salt and pepper to taste. Add the mushrooms, if you are using them, and the chicken. Serves 6.

CHICKEN PAPRIKA

2 3-lb. fryers
2 tsp. salt
1 tsp. paprika
½ cup butter
1 pt. sour cream
1 grated onion
1 tbsp. Worcestershire sauce

Flour
Pepper
Ginger
2 cups chicken stock or
   water
2 tbsp. chili sauce

Cut chickens into pieces for serving. Sprinkle with flour, mixed with salt, pepper, paprika, and ginger. Sauté in butter until brown. Add stock, Worcestershire sauce, chili sauce, and onion. Cover and cook slowly for 1½ hours. Skim off any surplus fat and add sour cream. Cook until the chicken is tender. If necessary, thicken gravy with 1 tbsp. flour mixed with 1 tbsp. water. Serves 6.

BROILED DEVILED CHICKEN

Split a broiler down the back, clean it, and dry it well. Season the chicken with salt and brush it with butter. Cook in a moderately hot oven (400°) for 10-15 minutes, or just long enough to make the flesh firm and give the skin a slight golden color.

Cream 2 or 3 tbsp. butter with 1 tsp. English mustard, a little cayenne pepper, and a few drops of Worcestershire sauce. Mix it with 1 cup of fine fresh bread crumbs. Remove the chicken from the oven and take out any bones that can be easily withdrawn. Spread the skin sides of the chicken with the mixture and broil the crumbed sides under medium heat for 20-25 minutes. Keep the broiling heat low enough so that the crumbs do not brown too much but have a nice golden color. Turn carefully to keep the crust intact. Serve hot or allow to cool, but never chill in the refrigerator.

CHICKEN CREPES AU CARI

4 8-oz. chicken breasts,   3 tbsp. butter
   cooked (save the stock)   1 cup flour
4 cups chicken stock   ½ tbsp. curry powder
3 pineapples, diced   Salt
2 ripe bananas, cut in fourths   White pepper
6 French Crêpes (see below)   1 chicken cube
8 cups cold water

Boil chicken breasts in the cold water until tender. Take off bone and save the stock; cut the chicken in small pieces. In another pot, melt butter and blend flour for 3 minutes. Add 4 cups chicken stock, curry powder, salt, pepper, bananas, chicken, pineapple, and chicken cube. Cook for 10 minutes. Set aside for 20 minutes. Stuff the crêpes and place in a baking dish. Take remainder of sauce and pour over the crêpes. Bake in oven at 375° for 10-12 minutes. Serves 6.

FRENCH CREPES

1 cup flour   1 oz. vanilla extract
1 oz. oil   1 cup half & half
1 cup milk   2 eggs
1 tsp. salt

Mix eggs into the flour. Add salt, oil, and vanilla and mix well. Add half & half and milk; beat until smooth. Pour small amount of batter onto a hot oiled 8-inch frying pan or crêpe pan. Brown on both sides over high heat. Remove from pan. Cover with towel and set aside. Makes 8 crêpes.

CHICKEN CREPES VERONIQUE

6 6-oz. poached chicken
  breasts
3 medium mushrooms,
  chopped
⅓ lb. butter
3 oz. green pepper sauce
2 cups Vermouth wine
3 oz. mozzarella cheese
3 oz. chicken base
⅓ tsp. bay leaf powder

½ qt. chicken stock
½ bunch green onions
2 oz. all-purpose flour
⅓ tsp. curry powder
4 egg yolks
1 tsp. mustard
1 tsp. salt
10 French Crêpes
Hollandaise Sauce

In a sauté pan, melt butter. Add chopped mushrooms and chopped green onions. Add flour and cook 3-5 minutes. Add chicken stock; mix well. Add chicken base, bay leaf powder, salt, mustard, curry powder, cheese, Vermouth wine, and green pepper sauce. Cook for 10 minutes. Add sliced chicken breast with skin off. Mix all together. Add egg yolks and roll in crêpes. Place each one on plate. Cover with Hollandaise Sauce, and brown under broiler, and serve. Serves 10.

CHICKEN BAKED IN SOUR CREAM

1 3-lb. frying chicken cut in
  serving pieces
½ tsp. grated lemon rind
½ onion, chopped
1 tsp. paprika
2 tsp. chopped parsley

3 tbsp. flour
1 cup sour cream
2 oz. sherry wine
1 cup chicken stock
Salt and pepper
3 tbsp. butter

Melt butter in large pan. Brown pieces of chicken slowly on all sides. Transfer chicken to baking casserole and add onion to skillet in which chicken was fried. Sauté slowly—blend in flour until smooth. Add stock and wine. Cook, stirring constantly until mixture thickens and boils. Add paprika, lemon rind, salt and pepper to taste, and sour cream. Pour sauce over chicken, cover, and bake in a 350° oven until tender. Before serving, add chopped parsley. Serves 4.

CHICKEN FRICASSEE

This is an old Creole recipe which is made in a brown sauce or cream sauce. I prefer the brown sauce. Chicken is something I cook often. There are so many ways to do it, and fricassee is a special dish. You'll love when it's done the Creole way. First, you have to brown your chicken, but not in oil. You brush the chicken with butter, turn the oven to 475°, and let brown on both sides.

¼ lb. butter
1 tbsp. salt
1 tsp. pepper
1 rib celery, chopped
½ cup pearl onions
1 cup white wine
½ cup green peas, frozen
½ medium bell pepper,
  chopped

4 cups water
2 tbsp. shortening
2 tbsp. flour
½ medium yellow onion,
  chopped
½ bunch green onions,
  chopped
2 bay leaves
2 3½ lb. fryers

Cut chicken into serving pieces. Sprinkle with salt and pepper. Place on a sheet pan. Melt butter and brush the chicken. Put in a preheated oven (450°) until brown on both sides; set aside. In a saucepan heat shortening with flour to make roux. Once it is brown, add onion, green onions, celery, bell pepper, water, bay leaves, white wine, green peas, and pearl onions. Pour this sauce over the chicken, put back into oven, and reduce the heat to 350°. Do not cover. Cook for 15-20 minutes. Serve with steamed rice. Serves 6.

CHICKEN FRICASSEE WITH BROWN SAUCE

1 6-7 lb. stewing hen
3 medium onions, minced
2 bay leaves, crushed
2 tbsp. minced celery
2 tsp. salt
1 tbsp. Worcestershire
  sauce
Dash cayenne pepper or
  Tabasco sauce

2 tbsp. lard or bacon fat
2 tbsp. flour
2 sprigs thyme
½ tsp. paprika
2 tbsp. minced parsley
½ tsp. pepper
½ bell pepper, chopped
2½ cups water

The successful chicken fricassee must have plenty of chicken, so get a large stewing hen. Have it cut up at the joints. Save the liver and gizzard. A 6 or 7 lb. fowl will serve 6 to 8 dinner guests. Wash the chicken pieces thoroughly and put in a Dutch oven with lard or bacon fat. Let simmer until brown, then take the chicken out and set it aside.

Brown the minced onions in grease. Add paprika. Stir in and brown the flour. Put the chicken back in the pot with water, bay leaves, thyme, cayenne, parsley, salt, celery, bell pepper, Worcestershire sauce, and pepper. Chop up the chicken gizzard and liver and add. Cook for 1 hour or until chicken is tender. Serve in a bowl or tureen, along with the rich gravy, and serve boiled rice as an accompaniment. Serves 6-8.

SAUTEED CHICKEN SUPREME

2 broilers (cut into serving
  pieces)
1 stick butter
2 tbsp. hot brandy
1 tsp. tomato paste
2 tbsp. flour
1 cup chicken stock
  (bouillon)

1 carton sour cream (¾ to
  1 cup)
2 tbsp. grated Parmesan
  cheese
1 grated lemon rind
Salt, red and black pepper
  to taste

Brown chicken all over in hot butter (slowly to prevent sticking). Pour over the brown chicken the hot brandy. Remove chicken from the pan and stir in tomato paste and flour; then pour in stock. Stir over heat until mixture comes to a boil; then beat in slowly with a whisk the sour cream, grated cheese, grated lemon rind, salt, and pepper. Place pieces of chicken into sauce and simmer gently for 40 minutes. Remove and arrange on serving dish. Pour some sauce over and pass the rest of the sauce in gravy boat. Serves 4-6 depending on size and number of pieces of chicken. Always serve this with rice. The gravy is delicious!

CHICKEN CREOLE

1 3½-lb. frying chicken	6 chopped shallots or ½
¼ cup olive oil	cup minced onion
2 tbsp. butter or margarine	5 tbsp. chopped bell
Few grains pepper	pepper
Few grains cayenne	1 tbsp. flour
1 sprig thyme	½ cup white wine
1 tbsp. minced parsley	1 can (1 lb. 4 oz.) tomatoes
1 bay leaf	1 tsp. salt

Disjoint chicken. Wipe pieces with damp cloth. Sauté in olive oil, turning to brown both sides. Combine tomatoes and 1 tbsp. butter; simmer 10 minutes, stirring occasionally. Add salt, pepper, and cayenne; cook 10 minutes. Add thyme, parsley, and bay leaf and cook 15 minutes or until sauce is thick.

Melt in remaining butter, blend in flour; cook until brown. Add chopped shallots and bell pepper; brown slightly. Add wine, stirring constantly, until slightly thickened. Add chicken. Cover; simmer 45 minutes or until chicken is tender. If desired, place chicken on hot cooked rice. Serves 4.

TURKEY WINGS

Restaurants serve so many turkeys during holidays that a lot of turkey wings are left over. So I learned how to make a dish out of them. They are good for making stock, of course, but I came up with this delicious entree too. Turkey wings have a lot of flavor, so the sauce is wonderful in this dish.

6 turkey wings	Salt
1 cup flour	Pepper
1½ qt. chicken stock	Thyme
½ white onion	2 bay leaves
2 pieces celery	2 cups oil

Cut turkey wings in half and wash in cold water, then dry with a cloth. Salt and pepper them. Then dust them in the flour. In a roasting pan add the oil. Place the turkey wings in the pan. Put in oven at 450° and cook until brown (45 minutes to 1 hour). Chop the onion and celery; add to the turkey wings, along with bay leaves, thyme, and chicken stock. Cover and cook at 350° for 1 hour and 45 minutes, or until tender. Serves 6.

ROAST TURKEY

1 14-15 lb. turkey	1 large yellow onion, finely chopped
2 tbsp. butter	½ lb. salt pork
1 cup port wine	1 cup oil
Salt and pepper	6 cups chicken stock or water
½ cup chestnuts	3 slices bread
½ tsp. dried thyme	½ cup milk
1 tsp. chopped green onions	1 lb. sausage meat
1 tsp. chopped parsley	

Prepare the following stuffing for the turkey. Make a slit in the shell of each chestnut on the flat side with a sharp knife. Put into a shallow pan with oil and cook in a hot oven at 400° for 5 minutes. Remove and when cool enough to handle, take off the shells and inner skin. Cook in chicken stock or water until soft, about 20 to 30 minutes. Soak bread in milk in a large mixing bowl. Cook sausage meat until browned. Remove with a slotted spoon and put into the bowl. Sauté yellow onion. Drain the chestnuts and put through a strainer. Add to the sausage with the onion, sausage fat, parsley, green onions, thyme, salt, and pepper.

Put into the turkey and secure with small skewers and string. Spread butter all over the turkey. Cover the breast and legs with thin slices of salt pork, place breast side up on a rack in a roasting pan, and put some slices of salt pork over the back. Cover with aluminum foil. Roast in a moderate oven at 350° for about 15 minutes to the pound.

An hour before the roast is due to be done, remove the aluminum foil. Put wine into the pan and baste every 15 minutes with the pan juices. Turkey is done when the juice runs clear after piercing a fork into the leg, or when the meat thermometer inserted in the leg registers 190°. Serves 8-10.

TURKEY POULETTE

1 lb. sliced turkey	**½ cup butter**
8 oz. mushroom stems and pieces	**4 slices toast, cut in half**
½ cup sherry wine	**2 pieces pimento, chopped**
8 slices bacon, cooked	**4 oz. grated Parmesan cheese**
1 tsp. pepper	**3 pt. milk**
6 chicken bouillon cubes	**1 cup flour**

Put butter in pot to melt. Add flour and mix well. Add hot milk, reduce heat, and add mushrooms, pimentos, pepper, sherry wine, and chicken bouillon.

Place 1 piece of toast on each plate and put a slice of turkey on top. Then put the sauce over the turkey and sprinkle the grated Parmesan cheese over. Bake in oven at 350° for 5-8 minutes. Top with 2 slices of cooked bacon and serve. Serves 4.

TURKEY AND OYSTER POULETTE

1 qt. oysters, drained
2 lb. cooked white turkey
   meat
¼ lb. butter
½ bunch green onions
½ gallon chicken stock
2 bay leaves
1 cup half & half cream

Dash thyme
½ cup dry white wine
3 oz. flour
½ cup sliced fresh
   mushrooms
3 egg yolks
Salt and pepper to taste
½ tsp. Worcestershire sauce

Dice turkey breast and boil with oysters in the chicken stock. Add bay leaves, salt, pepper, thyme, and Worcestershire. Let this come to a boil. Skim off the top. In another pan, add the butter, mushrooms, and green onions, and sauté for 5 minutes, then add flour. Cook for 3 minutes, then mix in turkey and oyster stock. Cook for 5 minutes, then add the wine, egg yolks, and cream. Stir and serve. Serves 10.

BAKED TURKEY

Thaw turkey, rinse well, and drain. Salt and pepper the cavity and stuff loosely. Rub the skin with oil or shortening, especially around the legs and wings so that it will brown evenly. Also cover the bird with a light cloth moistened in melted butter and hot water and permit it to brown slowly. Remove the cloth during the latter part of the baking. Trussing the bird keeps it in good shape. The following schedule can be used as a guide.

Oven temperature 325°.
6-8 lb. turkey—4½ to 4 hours
8-12 lb. turkey—4 to 4½ hours
12-16 lb. turkey—4½ to 5½ hours
16-20 lb. turkey—5½ to 7 hours
20-24 lb. turkey—7 to 8½ hours

PECAN STUFFING

1 large onion, finely minced
Turkey giblets, cooked and
  finely chopped
1½ tsp. salt
1 bay leaf
1 (7 oz.) can mushroom
  stems and pieces

2 eggs, well beaten
¼ cup butter or margarine
3 cups bread crumbs
½ tsp. pepper
¼ tsp. dried thyme
2 tbsp. minced parsley
1½ cups chopped pecans

Sauté onion in butter or margarine until light brown. Add giblets, bread crumbs, salt, pepper, thyme, bay leaf, parsley, mushrooms with liquid, and chopped pecans. Blend well, then add eggs and mix thoroughly. Makes enough to stuff a 12 to 15 lb. turkey.

DUCK A L'ORANGE

4 lb. duck, cut in half
½ cup currant jelly
1 bay leaf
1 whole black peppercorn

Rind of ½ lemon, grated
1½ cups brown gravy
Juice of 2 oranges
Rind of 1 orange, grated

Roast duck and make a brown gravy. Melt currant jelly in a saucepan; add bay leaf, peppercorn, ½ cup brown gravy, orange juice and rind, and lemon rind. Let boil for 10 minutes on a low heat. Add 1 cup more of brown gravy and boil. Strain and pour over ducks. Garnish with parboiled orange rind strips, and preserved kumquats or skinned orange sections. Serves 2.

ROAST DUCK

Rub duck, inside and out, with salt mixed with grated clove of garlic, pepper, paprika, and a few grains of ginger. Fill with stuffing and roast in an uncovered pan in a slow oven (325°), allowing 20 to 30 minutes per pound. Prick the fat skin with a fork from time to time. Serve with giblet gravy.

WILD RICE AND MUSHROOM STUFFING

½ lb. mushrooms, sliced   Salt and pepper
1 cup wild rice   2 tbsp. butter

Cook rice in boiling water until not completely tender. Sauté mushrooms in the butter. Add to the rice and season.

ROAST PIGEONS WITH RICE PILAU

6 slices bacon   ¾ cup chopped celery
1 onion, chopped   2 cups uncooked rice
4 cups chicken stock   4 eggs
Salt and pepper   4 pigeons
Mustard pickle juice

Dice bacon and fry until crisp. Remove bacon and brown celery and onion in drippings. Boil rice in chicken stock until tender. Add bacon, celery, and onion. Beat eggs and add rice. Season with salt and pepper. Dress pigeons, fill with rice mixture, and place on mounds of remaining rice. Bake in slow oven (325°) 45-60 minutes, basting frequently with mustard pickle juice. Serves 4.

ROCK CORNISH HENS CERISE

Get four 14-oz. Rock Cornish game hens (if they're frozen, let them thaw out). Wipe them inside and out with a cloth soaked in brandy, then sprinkle the cavities with seasoned salt. Let them stand while making the stuffing. In a heavy saucepan melt 2 tbsp. butter and when hot add ⅓ cup each chopped onions and chopped bell pepper, and 1 cup packaged precooked rice. Cook over low heat, stirring constantly until rice is lightly browned.

Combine ½ tsp. salt, ¼ tsp. diced oregano, and ¾ cup boiling condensed bouillon and add to the rice mixture. Heat all to boiling point, then cover, remove from heat, and let stand 15 minutes. Then mix in ½ cup chopped maraschino cherries (about 20 cherries). Fill the cavities of the Rock Cornish hens with the cherry stuffing, fasten with toothpicks or poultry pins, and arrange the hens on a rack in a shallow roasting pan.

Combine ¼ cup butter, melted, and 2 tbsp. maraschino cordial for a basting sauce and brush hens with this mixture. Roast hens at 425° for 50 minutes, or according to directions on packaged frozen Rock Cornish hens. Baste the hens frequently with the cherry-butter mixture during roasting. Serves 4.

BAKED QUAIL A LA CHEF LOUIS

6 small quail	¼ cup chopped onions
2 tbsp. unsalted butter	½ cup boiling stock or
2 tbsp. butter	water
¼ cup chopped carrots or	Toast
celery	Parsley for garnish

Rub quail with unsalted butter. Truss them with string. Place them on a broiler under low heat. Cook them 12-20 minutes, according to their size. Turn them frequently. Melt butter in a saucepan. Add and sauté vegetables for 1 minute. Add quail and sauté them until they are brown.

Add stock or water. Cover the quail with waxed paper. Place them in a moderate oven (350°) for 20 minutes. Serve them on toast. Garnish quail with parsley.

DEVILED SQUABS

Cut slashes in 4 dressed squabs, rub in mustard and cayenne, and broil squabs. Cream ½ cup butter, add 2 tsp. mustard, 2 tsp. Worcestershire sauce, ¼ tsp. pepper, dash cayenne, and ¼ tsp salt. Spread over broiled squabs just before serving.

STEWED RABBIT A LA CREOLE

2 young rabbits, cut up
3 cloves garlic, chopped
1 medium yellow onion, chopped
2 cups flour
1 tsp. white pepper
1 tbsp. thyme
1 qt. chicken stock

3 bay leaves
½ medium bell pepper, chopped
1 rib celery, chopped
1 cup shortening
1 tbsp. salt
1 cup diced tomatoes

Salt and pepper the rabbits; dust in flour. Melt shortening in a heavy skillet. When the shortening is hot, put the rabbits in. Brown on both sides then take out and set aside. Remove most of the shortening; add chopped garlic, onion, celery, and bell pepper. Cook for 5 to 8 minutes. Add diced tomatoes, bay leaves, and thyme. If the skillet can't hold all of the rabbits, get a large pan and put the rabbit and everything else in skillet. Add the chicken stock and place in oven at 350° for 30 minutes. Do not cover. Serves 6-8.

Desserts

In New Orleans, desserts have to be good, just as it is with a cup of coffee. I think bread pudding might be the most popular dessert in New Orleans. There are a number of ways to prepare it. You will find a couple in this book, one with meringue and one with whiskey sauce, for example. One of the first things I learned to cook was bread pudding.

Caramel cup custard has been around longer than I can remember. Rice custard is not very familiar to most restaurants, though. A fine old recipe is Pot à la Crème Chocolate. This you will find at Kabby's in the Hilton. And Bananas Foster is an old dessert flambé.

I hope you will find some recipes that you can use from time to time. I guess we can talk about desserts for an hour, but we have other things for you at Kabby's. I have Mile-High Ice-Cream Pie, Mississippi Mud Pie, and others on the dessert cart. In New Orleans you forget the calories and just eat and drink. If you've never been here before, you don't want to miss anything.

POT A LA CREME CHOCOLATE

2 cups half & half
2 oz. bittersweet chocolate
Pinch salt
½ cup sugar

8 egg yolks
6 oz. semisweet chocolate
2 pt. whipped cream

Heat half & half. Put bittersweet chocolate and semisweet chocolate over double boiler. Add salt. Take off heat when chocolate melts. Fold in egg yolks, one at a time. Let cool. Put in refrigerator. To make whipped cream, whip cream in mixer on medium speed. Add sugar. Whip until stiff. Top chocolate mixture with whipped cream, and serve in chocolate cup or custard cup. Serves 4-6.

CHOCOLATE SOUFFLE

6 tbsp. butter
1¼ cups sugar
1½ tsp. vanilla flavoring
6 tbsp. flour
9 eggs, separated

6 tbsp. hot water
5 squares unsweetened
   chocolate
5 cups milk
Pinch salt

Melt the chocolate over hot, but not boiling, water. Add the sugar and hot water and stir until smooth. In another pan, melt the butter, add flour, and gradually stir in the milk. Bring to boiling point, stirring constantly. Remove from the heat. Combine with the chocolate mixture; add salt. Beat the egg yolks until thick and add to the chocolate mixture. Cool. Fold in stiffly beaten egg whites and vanilla flavoring. Set in a pan of warm water and bake for 25 minutes at 375°. Serves 12.

PROFITEROLES AU CHOCOLAT

¾ cup butter
1¾ cups granulated sugar
2½ cups heavy whipping
   cream
2 tsp. Cognac

1 cup water
1 cup flour
4 eggs
4 oz. cooking chocolate

Melt ½ cup of butter, add water, and bring to a boil. Remove from the stove, add the sifted flour all at once, and stir vigorously until blended. Stir in 1 tsp. of sugar and put back on over very low heat, stirring constantly until the mixture is dry and leaves small traces of dried dough on the bottom of the saucepan. Take off heat and add the eggs, one by one, beating after each one, until the mixture is smooth.

Drop this cream puff pastry by teaspoons onto a buttered and lightly floured baking sheet. Bake 35-40 minutes in a moderate oven (350°) until a light golden color. Remove from the oven and cool. Whip 1½ cups of cream until thick but not dry and stir in 2 tbsp. of sugar. Make a small hole in the bottom of each puff and force in the whipped cream with help of a pastry tube. Make a pyramid of cream puffs on a dessert platter.

Melt the chocolate with the remaining sugar and butter in the top of a double boiler; stir in the remaining cup of cream and the Cognac. Pour the hot fudge sauce over the cream puff pyramid and serve hot. Makes 2 dozen.

CHOCOLATE MINT BOMBE

1 qt. chocolate ice cream
2 egg whites
¼ cup granulated sugar

½ tsp peppermint extract
1 cup whipped heavy cream
½ tsp. green coloring

Line *stainless steel* bowl with most of the chocolate ice cream and freeze. Beat egg whites stiff to a peak. Add sugar while beating. Whip cream and add the egg whites. Then stir in peppermint and green coloring. Fill center, freeze. Top what will be the bottom with remaining chocolate ice cream and freeze. Serves up to 12.

THE PONTCHARTRAIN'S CHOCOLATE SAUCE

3 qt. breakfast cream
6 cups sugar
20 squares bitter chocolate

20 bars German sweet chocolate

Dissolve sugar in cream. Over double boiler add all chocolate to sugar and cream and stir as it melts (about 15 minutes). Makes 1 gallon. Pour this sauce over slices of bombe to serve.

RICE CUSTARD

8 eggs
1 tsp. nutmeg
1 lb. sugar
1 tsp. vanilla extract

1 qt. milk
1 cup raisins
3 cups rice

Mix sugar, milk, eggs, nutmeg, and vanilla extract together. Then add raisins and rice and pour in baking dish. Bake for 1 hour in oven at 325°. Serves 6-8.

BREAD PUDDING

6 hard dinner rolls
8 whole eggs
2 cups sugar
3 tsp. vanilla flavor
1 cup orange juice

½ lb. melted butter
1½ cups raisins
1 qt. milk
Whiskey Sauce (see below)

Dice dinner rolls in small pieces and place in a bowl. In a mixing bowl, combine eggs, milk, sugar, vanilla, orange juice, butter, and raisins. Pour over bread and place in a baking dish. Bake at 350° for 45 minutes to 1 hour. Pour Whiskey Sauce over Bread Pudding and serve hot. Serves 8-10.

WHISKEY SAUCE

2 eggs
1 pt. milk
½ tsp. vanilla flavor
½ cup whiskey
⅓ tsp. cinnamon

⅓ tsp. nutmeg
½ cup sugar
2 tbsp. cornstarch
1 cup cold water

Mix all ingredients together except cornstarch and water and put over double boiler until hot. Add cornstarch and water.

CREOLE BREAD PUDDING

3 cups French bread cubes
  (day-old bread)
2 eggs, separated
1¼ cups milk
¼ tsp. cream of tartar

¼ cup raisins
2 tbsp. butter
6 tbsp. sugar
1 tsp. vanilla
4 tbsp. sugar

Moisten bread cubes with water; squeeze to remove excess water. Stir in raisins and softened butter; pour into greased 1-quart casserole. Beat egg yolks and 6 tbsp. sugar; add milk and vanilla. Pour over bread mixture. Bake in 350° oven for 45 minutes.

To make meringue, beat egg whites and cream of tartar until soft peaks form when beaters are lifted. While continuing to beat, gradually add 4 tbsp. sugar. Spoon meringue over pudding; return to oven for 15 minutes. Serves 6.

Variation: Before spooning meringue over pudding, quickly spread a thin layer of strawberry preserves or orange marmalade.

BREAD AND BUTTER PUDDING

1 qt. milk
6 oz. sugar
Pinch salt
Pinch vanilla flavor

10 slices sandwich bread
6 oz. hot butter
12 oz. of eggs
20 oz. coffee cream

Cut bread slices into small cubes and toast them in oven until they get golden brown. When removed from the oven sprinkle with hot butter until bread cubes are well soaked with the butter. Then place the bread cubes in individual molds or in one large one. Mix remaining ingredients. Pour custard mix over bread and bake in water bath at 400° about 45 minutes until custard firms. Serves 6-8.

PIE DOUGH

1 lb. all-purpose flour
1 oz. salt

½ lb. shortening
½ pt. ice water

Mix flour and shortening with salt then add water drop by drop until all has been mixed. Then roll out.

RUM PIE

9" cooked pie shell
6 egg yolks
1 envelope gelatin
½ cup dark rum

1 cup sugar
1 pt. cream
½ cup cold water

Beat egg yolks until light, then add sugar. Meanwhile, soak gelatin in cold water. Put gelatin and water over low heat and bring it to a boil. Pour over sugar-egg mixture stirring briskly. Whip cream until stiff. Fold into the mixture. Flavor with dark rum and cook until thick. Pour into pie shell and cook in 350° oven for 45 minutes to 1 hour.

MISSISSIPPI MUD PIE

1 hotel pan with baked
  chocolate cake
12 oz. miniature
  marshmallows

1 square sweetened
  chocolate
2 cans evaporated milk
½ lb. pecans

Top cake with marshmallows. Place in oven and lightly brown the marshmallows. Melt chocolate, add evaporated milk and pecans, and mix well. Pour mixture and spread over the top of the marshmallows. Let the cake cool and then serve in small portions. Serves 40.

MILE-HIGH ICE-CREAM PIE

This is a famous dessert. When I arrived at the Pontchartrain they were serving ice-cream pie. They used vanilla and chocolate ice cream. In late 1969, I became executive chef, and in 1972 I changed the pie to include chocolate, vanilla, and peppermint. The ice-cream pie is now served at Kabby's with these three flavors.

1½ cups sifted flour
½ tsp. salt
¼ cup shortening
4-5 tbsp. cold water
1 pt. vanilla ice cream
1 pt. peppermint ice cream

½ tsp. vanilla
½ cup sugar
1 pt. chocolate ice cream
8 egg whites
¼ tsp. cream of tartar
Chocolate Sauce (see below)

Sift together flour and salt for crust. Cut in shortening until pieces are the size of small peas. Sprinkle 1 tablespoon of cold water over flour mixture and gently toss with fork. Repeat until all is moistened. Form into a ball with fingers and roll out to ⅛" thickness on lightly floured surface. Fit loosely into a 9-inch pie pan, pricking well. Bake 10-12 minutes at 450°. Cool.

Layer ice cream in pie shell. Beat egg whites with vanilla and cream of tartar until soft peaks form. Gradually add sugar, beating until stiff and glossy and sugar is dissolved. Spread meringue over ice cream to edges of pastry. Broil 30 seconds to 1 minute to brown meringue. Freeze at least several hours. Drizzle Chocolate Sauce over each serving. Serves 8-10.

CHOCOLATE SAUCE

1 qt. half & half
3 cups granulated sugar
10 squares bitter chocolate

10 squares German sweet
chocolate

Cook all sauce ingredients in a double boiler until thick, using only half of cream to start with. Add the balance of cream to achieve pouring consistency.

LEMON ICEBOX PIE

4 cans condensed milk
8 egg yolks
6 egg whites
1 tsp. lemon flavor

2 cups lemon juice
1 orange rind
½ lb. powdered sugar
2 baked pie shells (9")

Put condensed milk in mixing bowl. Add lemon juice, lemon flavor, and egg yolks; mix well. Pour in pie shells and put in freezer. Let set until it gets hard.

In mixing bowl, beat egg whites until the meringue rises. Add powdered sugar. Mix until foamy, then add orange rind. Put the meringue over each pie and bake in oven at 450° until meringue turns light brown. Put back in freezer for 4-6 hours and serve. Makes 2 pies.

BANANA SPLIT PIE

2 eggs, well beaten
1½ cups powdered sugar
1 stick margarine, room
   temperature
1 oz. sweetened chocolate,
   grated

3 bananas
Lemon or pineapple juice
1 baked 9" pie shell
Whipped dessert topping
Chopped nuts

Combine powdered sugar, eggs, and margarine and beat with an electric mixer about 5 minutes until fluffy. Add grated chocolate and mix well. Pour into cooled, baked shell. Dip bananas in lemon or pineapple juice to prevent darkening. Then thinly slice bananas and arrange on pie. Chill 2 hours. Just before serving, top with whipped dessert topping and chopped nuts.

CREME DELERY

3 pkg. cream cheese　　　　**2 tbsp. sugar**
1 cup heavy cream　　　　　　**1 tbsp. vanilla (optional)**

Take cream cheese out of the refrigerator and warm to room temperature. Crush in a mixing bowl with a fork.

Work in ½ cup heavy cream, a little at a time, beating with a fork. Pour in the second ½ cup of cream and beat uninterruptedly for about 3 minutes with a rotary beater.

Add sugar and vanilla (optional). Beat once more with the rotary beater. Pour the sauce into a serving bowl and set in the refrigerator until ready to serve. Just before serving, stir vigorously with a spoon, as the wait in the refrigerator has a tendency to thicken the sauce a little more than is desirable. Use this cream over fruit.

BANANAS FOSTER

½ lb. light brown sugar　　　**1 tsp. ground cinnamon**
2 oz. granulated sugar　　　　**¼ lb. butter**
4 medium-ripe bananas,　　　**1 cup banana liqueur**
　split in half　　　　　　　　**4 cups vanilla ice cream**
1½ oz. rum

In pan, melt butter, brown sugar, and white sugar. Cook for 5-10 minutes. Add bananas and roll them in the sugar mix. Add banana liqueur and cook 10 minutes. Add the rum and flame. Add cinnamon while rum is flaming (the cinnamon will sparkle). Serve over vanilla ice cream. Serves 4.

PECAN PIE

12 eggs

¾ cups vanilla

Pinch salt

3 cups sugar

4 cups dark karo syrup

3 cups pecans

1½ cups butter, melted

Unbaked pie shell

Mix all ingredients together—eggs first, then sugar, butter, vanilla, syrup, pecans, and salt. Place in raw pie shell and bake at 350° until set (1 hour and 15 minutes).

THE PONTCHARTRAIN'S FRUIT TARTS

Use assorted fruits—peaches, apricots, pears, pineapple, cherries, and bananas. Use canned fruits if fresh are not available. Be sure to get home-style peaches if canned. Arrange the fruit in layers in a baking dish. Sprinkle each layer with brown sugar, slivered almonds, and dabs of sweet butter. Pour ½ cup sherry, or more if you make a large amount, over all and cover with crushed macaroons. Bake 20 minutes at 350°.

CHERRIES JUBILEE

1 qt. vanilla ice cream

5 dozen pitted bing
  cherries, drained

¾ cup brandy

Zests of 1 orange

3 tbsp. powdered sugar

2 tbsp. curaçao

Divide ice cream into 8 portions in well-chilled dessert dishes. Cut thin shavings from the surface of the skin of the orange and shred them very fine to make the orange zests. Combine them with cherries and sugar in a shallow saucepan or chafing dish. Add curaçao, then add the brandy. Ignite and pour the flaming fruit over the ice cream. Serves 8.

COCA-COLA CAKE

2 cups flour
2 cups sugar
2 sticks butter
1 cup Coca-Cola
3 tbsp. cocoa
½ cup buttermilk

2 eggs, beaten
1 tsp. baking soda
1 tsp. vanilla
2 cups miniature
  marshmallows

Combine flour and sugar, mixing well. Heat butter and Coca-Cola and bring to the boiling point. Pour over flour and sugar. Add buttermilk, eggs, cocoa, baking soda, and vanilla. Mix well. Then add marshmallows and pour into a 9" x 13" greased cake pan. Bake for 30 to 35 minutes at 350°. The marshmallows will rise to the top during the baking.

ICING

1 stick butter
6 tbsp. Coca-Cola
1 box powdered sugar

1 tsp. vanilla
1 tbsp. cocoa
1 cup toasted pecans

Mix and spread on cooled cake.

CHOCOLATE ICEBOX CAKE

4 squares German sweet
  chocolate
8 tbsp. water
8 eggs
½ pt. whipping cream

2 squares baker's bitter
  chocolate
8 tbsp. sugar
2 pkg. ladyfingers

Cream egg yolks and sugar. Melt chocolate in water and add to yolk and sugar mixture. Beat egg whites stiff and add to above when cool. Line springform pan with ladyfingers, bottom and sides. Add layer of chocolate mixture and dabs of whipped cream. Add few bits of ladyfingers, then more chocolate and cream. Freezes well. Serves 14 generously.

RUM CAKE

½ cup chopped pecans
1 (4 oz.) pkg. vanilla instant
    pudding mix
½ cup water
4 eggs

1 (18½ oz.) pkg. golden
    butter cake mix
½ cup light rum
½ cup cooking oil
Hot Rum Glaze (see below)

Grease and flour a tube or bundt cake pan. Crumble nuts into bottom of pan. Place cake and pudding mixes into large mixing bowl. Add rum, water, oil, and eggs; beat 2 minutes. Pour batter into cake pan and bake at 325° for 50 to 60 minutes. Remove cake from oven and immediately pour on Hot Rum Glaze. Hot glaze will cause cake to settle but no cause for alarm, for the cake will still taste delicious. Cool cake in pan for 30 minutes and remove to serving plate. (To make a chocolate rum cake, substitute a fudge butter cake mix and a package of chocolate instant pudding mix.)

HOT RUM GLAZE

1 cup sugar
¼ cup light rum

1 stick butter
¼ cup water

Place glaze ingredients in a small saucepan and boil for 2 to 3 minutes.

FLO'S COFFEE CAKE

½ cup butter
1½ cups flour
1 cup sugar
2 eggs

½ cup milk
1 tsp. vanilla
1 heaping tsp. baking
    powder

Cream butter. Sift flour several times and add to butter. Add sugar, eggs, and milk, mixing well. Then add vanilla and baking powder. Put batter in long cake pan and bake in preheated 325° oven. Make icing.

ICING

5 tbsp. melted butter
5 tbsp. brown sugar

3 tbsp. cream
1½ cups nuts

Cook butter, sugar, and cream a while, then add nuts. Spread over cake when cake is done and put under broiler at medium heat for a few seconds. Cut in squares and serve while hot.

RED VELVET CAKE

½ cup shortening
1½ cups sugar
2 eggs
2 tsp. cocoa
¼ cup red food coloring
1 tbsp. vinegar

1 tsp. salt
1 tsp. vanilla
1 cup buttermilk
2½ cups sifted flour
1 tsp. baking soda

Cream shortening and sugar until fluffy. Add eggs, one at a time; beat for 1 minute. Mix cocoa and food coloring to pastelike consistency; add with salt to sugar mixture. Combine vanilla and buttermilk; add slowly to sugar mixture, alternately with flour. Combine soda and vinegar; stir into batter, do not beat. Pour into 2 greased and floured 9" cake pans. Bake in 350° oven for 25-30 minutes. Cool and frost.

RED VELVET CAKE FROSTING

3 tbsp. flour
1 cup (2 sticks) butter
1 tsp. vanilla

1 cup milk
1 cup confectioners' sugar

Mix flour and milk to smooth paste. Cook over low heat until thick, stirring constantly. Cool. Cream butter, sugar, and vanilla. Add flour mixture gradually, beating constantly until you get a spreading consistency.

GINGERBREAD

½ cup shortening
2½ cups flour
½ tsp. salt
½ tsp. ground cloves
½ tsp. baking soda
2 eggs

½ cup sugar
1½ tsp. baking powder
1 tsp. ginger
1 cup karo syrup
1 tsp. cinnamon
1 cup water

Mix in mixing bowl the shortening, sugar, flour, salt, cloves, ginger, soda, cinnamon, baking powder, and syrup. Mix well, 3-4 minutes. Add water. Add eggs, one at a time. Bake in preheated oven at 350° for 45 minutes to 1 hour.

BLUEBERRY MUFFINS

16 eggs
¼ cup salt
½ lb. butter
12 lb. flour
1½ cups baking powder

2½ qt. sugar
3½ lb. shortening
1 gallon milk
1½ cups vanilla flavor
8 cups blueberries

Combine shortening, sugar, and eggs in mixing bowl. Beat for 10 minutes. Add flour and baking powder and beat for another 10 minutes. Then add milk, salt, vanilla flavor, and butter. Whip for 25 minutes. Fill muffin pans with mixture and place blueberries on top of each muffin. Bake at 375° for 45 minutes to 1 hour. Makes 12 dozen.

CREPES SOUFFLES

1 cup flour
1 oz. oil
2 eggs
1 oz. vanilla extract
2 cups half & half
2 cups homogenized milk
6 egg whites

¾ lb. confectioners' sugar
Rind of 1 orange, grated
5 egg yolks
½ cup granulated sugar
1 tsp. mace
2 oz. dark rum

To make crêpes, mix flour, oil, whole eggs, vanilla, 1 cup of the half & half, and the milk into a batter. Brown on a griddle, crêpe pan, or small fry pan.

Preheat oven to 400°. To make filling, mix egg whites with confectioners' sugar, using an egg beater or wire whisk to beat to a meringue texture. Add orange rind and beat until the mixture expands. Beat for an additional 10 minutes until dry and stiff peaks form. Fold into crêpes and place in oven for 10 minutes. They will rise like a soufflé.

To make the sauce, put egg yolks, granulated sugar, mace, and remainder of the half & half in a double boiler. Stir constantly for 10 to 15 minutes until sauce has thickened. Add rum. When crêpes have risen, remove from oven and arrange on serving plates. Cover with sauce and serve. Makes 8 crêpes.

PRALINE CREPES

8 crêpes
4 tbsp. brown sugar
½ cup Courvoisier
¾ lb. chopped pecans

½ lb. butter
2 cups praline liqueur
2 cups whipped cream

Melt butter in pan, add the sugar, and cook until light brown in color. Add praline liqueur and allow to reduce until a thick syrup. Add one crêpe at a time, folding into the syrup. Add the Courvoisier and flame. Place whipped cream over each crêpe. Sprinkle chopped pecans over whipped cream and serve. Serves 4.

CREPES KAHLUA

¾ cup butter
½ cup sugar
½ cup macaroon crumbs
½ cup Kahlua or other
  coffee-flavored liqueur

24 French crêpes (5 or 6"
  in diameter)
½ cup (¼ lb.) butter
1 pt. heavy cream, whipped
Additional Kahlua

Make filling by creaming together the ¾ cup butter, sugar, macaroon crumbs, and Kahlua. Spread mixture on crêpes and roll. When it's time to serve, heat crêpes in the ½ cup butter in a chafing dish or electric frying pan. Serve with whipped cream and a drizzle of Kahlua. Serves 12 (2 crêpes per serving).

PECAN LACE COOKIES

2 tbsp. butter
2 eggs, well beaten
½ cup pastry flour
1/16 tsp. salt
2 cups sugar

1 tsp. vanilla
1 tsp. baking powder
2 cups coarsely chopped
  pecans

Cream butter and sugar; add eggs and vanilla. Mix thoroughly and add flour, baking powder, salt, and pecans. Drop ½ teaspoons far apart on a buttered and floured tin. Bake in a hot oven (400°). Cool slightly before removing from pan.

Note: Do not attempt to make these in hot weather.

CORNMEAL WAFERS

1 cup white cornmeal
1 tsp. salt
1 to 2 tsp. grated onion
1 egg, beaten

1½ tsp. sugar
2½ tbsp. bacon drippings
  or butter
1½ cups boiling water

Preheat oven to 400°. Grease baking sheets. Mix the cornmeal, sugar, salt, bacon drippings or butter, and onions. Add the boiling water and stir until smooth. Add the egg and beat well. Drop by scant teaspoonfuls on baking sheets, about an inch apart. Flatten with the spoon and bake until crisp and brown around the edges, about 15 minutes. Makes about 50 wafers.

Almond Wafers: Add ¼ cup chopped almonds to batter. After the cakes have been flattened, garnish with slivered almonds.

DAINTY OATMEAL COOKIES

1 stick butter
1 egg
2 tsp. flour

1 cup sugar
1 tbsp. vanilla
1 cup oatmeal

Cream butter and sugar together; add vanilla, egg, oatmeal, and flour. Beat with a wooden spoon only until blended. Drop small balls from a demitasse spoon 2 inches apart on a foil-lined cookie sheet. Bake in preheated 350° oven for 12 to 15 minutes or until golden brown. Cool and take off pan. Makes 3 dozen.

BROWNIES

6½ cups flour
2 tsp. salt
20 eggs
4½ cups chopped pecans
10 cups sugar

10 tsp. vanilla
5 tsp. baking powder
3½ cups melted butter
10 squares unsweetened
    chocolate

Beat eggs well and add sugar. Melt chocolate and add it and flour to egg mixture. Add remaining ingredients and mix well together. Grease 12" x 48" sheet pan and bake in 350° oven for 1 hour. Serves 30.

PRALINE CANDY

1 cup brown sugar (packed
    lightly)
¾ cup corn syrup
1 tsp. vanilla

2 cups half & half
½ stick butter
2 cups broken pecans

Put sugar, half & half, syrup, and butter in pan and bring to a boil. (This must be a hard boil so that when tested in cold water it forms a hard ball.) When the mixture begins to boil, stir to keep from sticking and lower heat to prevent burning. When hard ball forms in water take off heat and add vanilla and pecans, mixing the pecans in well but stirring as little as possible. Butter a platter and drop from two teaspoons. Makes about 33 pralines. Let cool and wrap each one in waxed paper. *Be careful not to burn—lower heat while cooking.*

Index